The Night of the Cougar

Memories I Could Do Without

Order this book online at www.trafford.com
or email orders@trafford.com

Most Trafford titles are also available at major online book retailers.

Printed in Victoria, BC, Canada.

ISBN: 978-1-4269-0053-2 (SC)
ISBN: 978-1-4269-0054-9 (HC)
ISBN: 978-1-4269-0055-6 (EBOOK)

*Our mission is to efficiently provide the world's finest, most comprehensive book publishing
service, enabling every author to experience success. To find out how to publish your book, your
way, and have it available worldwide, visit us online at www.trafford.com*

Trafford rev. 5/10/2010

Trafford
PUBLISHING® www.trafford.com

North America & international
toll-free: 1 888 232 4444 (USA & Canada)
phone: 250 383 6864 ♦ fax: 812 355 4082

Readers comments

Western Horsemen Magazine:

Say, by any chance does Lyle Lybbert have any more memories he could do without? I just read the article in the November 69 issue and thought it was plenty funny one evening after supper I ventured reading aloud to my mom. Now, she's not the horse nut that I am, but she grew up on the farm and she and her sister were the only kids around who drove a horse and buggy to town to school – a fact of which they were ashamed since everybody else had cars, but they enjoyed it immensely. She learned the inns and outs of buggy driving: the former when they got stuck in the muddy ditches along their farmland. The latter when the horse pulled so hard to free the buggy that he jumped plumb out of his harness! Anyway, she always enjoyed some good country humor.

Now Mama was mixed in a batch of homemade bread when I start reading and it will be a wonder if those loafs are edible! The article was many times funnier when read aloud. We laughed until our sides ached, which wasn't any to hard with our stomach full with of a big meal; and it took us a good while to get through the reading as we choke so often and I had to stop regularly to wipe those tears of laughter away before I could go on.

The way the author embellished those tales made it the funniest piece I've read in a long time. If Mr. Lybbert has any more memories he's got to get rid of, we sure would appreciate it if he'd share them with Western Horsemen readers.

Mary E. Genges
Broomfield, Colorado 80020

Lybbert strikes again

Western Horsemen Magazine:

Thanks for the side splitting stories "Memories I Could do Without." This is a gem of American literature I'll give odds that old Mark Twain is plead his case before the high tribunal right now trying to get reincarnated so he can have a second chance after having been bested by Lybbert.

This was so good that I felt we western horsemen shouldn't hog it, so I requested that the editors of the Reader's Digest take a look and get a laugh, then let the rest of the world in on a good thing.

Gene Holder
Arrowhead Custom Leather
MacGregor Texas 76657

Along with these comments my dad also received a letter from another individual from Texas. In this letter this man ordered three more copies of dad's book. Along with the order he made this statement, "no one should ever be so foolish as to buy only one copy of this funny book. I made the mistake of buying a single copy, as I told my friends about this book of course they wanted to borrow it. And then others borrowed the book from them. It wasn't long until I lost total track of that single copy.

Please send me three copies of your book; one copy is to read and lend; the second copy is just to read and the third copy is to hide and keep very precious. Thank you!"

Forward

'MEMORIES I COUD DO WITHOUT', and other short stories is a series of short stories written at various times throughout the author's life. The majority of these stories have been previously published in other magazines. Magazines such as the Western Horsemen, Canadian Cattlemen, Field & Stream and Rodeo. However, some of these short stories had never been seen in print until dad's first book was put together. The setting for most of the stories is the Knight Ranch, which is located some 40 miles south of Lethbridge, Alberta, Canada. This ranch spreads out on top of what is known as the Milk River Ridge. At one time this ranch consisted of something like 300,000 acres; over time portions were sold and it now has 81,000 acres. The South border of the ranch is about 20 miles from the Canadian-US border. The town of Milk River, mentioned in one story, would be 25 miles east of the Knight Ranch and is located beside the highway that links Great Falls, Montana and Calgary, Alberta. This part of the Alberta is seldom referred to in history books, however, it is the setting for most of these stories.

Dad often mentioned how pleased he was with his second daughter, Linda Wolf who did the cartoons, especially the front cover. Linda loves sketching for a hobby but she has never had an art lesson in her life and is the southpaw besides. We think she did just fine, don't you?

Further acknowledgments: Elaine Lybbert a daughter in-law and dad's oldest daughter Annette Martin for able assistance as proofreaders. Other illustrations were taken from the etchings of Earl W. Bascom. Earl's story is also included in this book. As stated above the cartoons were done by Linda Wolf, and for this publication Julie Lybbert did the front cover in color using an original sketching by Linda Wolf.

Note: Inasmuch as my Dad gave me permission to re-publish his Dad's book I must note that I have added one story and one poem. Dean Lybbert

About the Author

Lyle R. Lybbert was born in the town of Raymond, Alberta, Canada on January 11, 1918. His father died one year after he was born in the flu epidemic of 1919. His mother passed away 10 years later leaving a family of seven children to fend for themselves. The oldest brother and sister, though scarcely more than children themselves, had married by then and made a home for the younger children until they could make it on their own.

Lyle's family was very horse oriented so Lyle just naturally gravitated to the Knight Ranch, one of the largest horse ranches in Canada at the time. The ranch was pretty much his home from the time he was 16 until he was married at the ripe old age of 19.

In the next three years Lyle and his wife Dorothy produced three children and then once the war was raging in Europe he joined the Canadian Army and for four years helped to fight the war that was to end all wars, while his beloved wife lived in a rented cold water flat with their children along with Dorothy's mother Bertha Oler.

Following the war, six more children were born, however three of them died shortly after birth causing much sorrow and anguish to the young parents. After they were starved off a sorry farm in the Brooks district Lyle went back to work as a ranch hand for a short

4

while, then he did 3 three years as a Municipal Policeman and finally ended up as a Primary Products Inspector for the Department of Agricultural, a division of the Alberta Government. His hobbies were writing, and riding fine horses. They had four sons and two daughters, now all married with 28 grandchildren and a load of great-grandchildren. Lyle passed away July 12, 2006.

Lybbert is pronounced Lib bert like the Statue of 'Liberty'.

Table Of Contents

Lyle R. Lybbert ... Cowboy – Author
By Carl Lybbert

Lyle's brother, Carl, author of this article, writes: "In reading my brothers articles in the Western Horsemen Magazine and the glowing reports submitted to the "Letters From Riders" section of the magazine, I thought your readers might be interested in learning something about the life of a Lyle Lybbert. I wrote for the Canadian Cattlemen's magazine for three years prior to moving from Canada to the Evergreen State in the U.S.A. Most of my work was on assignment and biographical in nature. It suddenly occurred to me that of all the biographies I had written, there are few more interesting than the life of my own brother. And if you don't think so after reading his story, then the fault will be mine."

Lyle Raymond Lybbert was born in the town of Raymond, Alberta, Canada, January 11, 1918. When he was scarcely a long yearling, he lost his father. When he was about eight, our family moved onto a ranch in Middle Coulee, where my brother Mel was to earn the living for our widowed mother and her children. That same year, Mel decided that Lyle should be a cowboy with the rest of the outfit; so he traded for a couple of yearning colts that were to be Lyle's remuda. Lyle named one of the colts Laddie and the other colt Two Step. He broke them to lead and ride all by himself. One day he had saddled Two Step to help Mel jingle the work horses. By now the gray colt was kid-gentle, and Lyle was resting his head on the colt's mane, waiting for Mel to curry his horse. Both Lyle and Two-Step were half asleep as Mel was concluded his task of currying. With a sly grin Mel stuck the curry comb beneath two steps tail as he walked past, were upon the colt clamped down with his tail and Two-Step came unwound. This was Lyle's first exhibition as a bronc rider and he did it up brown.

The following year we lost our mother, but a gentle sister and a noble brother-in-law took Lyle into their home along with an older brother and a sister and raised them as her own. The Snow outfit was mostly a horse ranch in those days and here Lyle learn how to handle horses. Mel decided that Laddie and Two Step were putting on too much weight for riding horses so he traded for a little quite mare for Lyle to ride. The mare was a true albino, and her eyes were white "all over" as Lyle put it. He named her Alby. The sunlight seemed to hurt her eyes, and when Lyle turner her out in the little pasture, where they kept the jingle ponies, she would often seek the shade of a large tree that grew in one corner of the field. She was exceedingly hard to catch, and Lyle was hard put to catcher by himself. One day he conceived of an idea; while Alby was dozing with eyes closed in the shade. Thus with all the stealth of the Comanche, Lyle climbed into the tree and jumped onto the mare's neck. Frightened nearly to death Alby bolted wildly, but my brother hung on for dear life. Finally Alby gave up and came to a standstill. From then on this became a standard procedure until Alby decided she'd rather brave the heat of the sun than the startling experience of being jumped on from a tree.

In 1932 my younger brother signed on with the huge Knight and Weston ranching Co. Ltd. His first job was that of a mule skinner. Along with Inj Betts and Harold Lee, he drove a 12 head hitched of half broke mules pulling a Rod Weeder. By mid-summer, however, Ray Knight had promoted all three boys to riding the range. At that time the Knight and Weston outfit ran close to 1,000 horses – mostly draft horses, but also a good number of light, well bred English Thoroughbreds. With close to 300 horses in the Remuda, Ray decided that no one would be allowed to ride any one horse more often than once a week, this was done in an effort to keep the whole remuda "rode down."

Lyle claims he walked home more times than the most virtuous bell in Western Canada. By fall, he said he was getting used to come home in camp on the same horse he went out on. Before the summer was out, these three boys were even trying out horses for the ranch's bucking string.

One day Knight and his foreman, Andy Newell, were watching as the boys riding out bucking horse after bucking horse. "By gosh Andy", said Knight "we've got to think of another way to try out the bucking horses – them boys are break in all my good bucking horses to ride."

With that thought in mind, Knight rig up a dummy saddle with a trip-cinch so he could pull the trip rope and allow the horse to buck off everything, thus building up a Bronc's confidence.

This was the introduction of the use of a dummy saddle in trying out bucking horses.

Ray Knight was known as the "Father of the Stampede" in Canada – he produced the first rodeo or stampede in Canada in 1902. He owned one of the best strings of bucking horses in the business. Ray Knight was also very influential in the Calgary stampede. Some believe the Calgary Stamped would not have succeeded with out Ray Knight. Many of his horses received national recognition – Slim Sweden, Easy Money, Lonely Valley, Grey, and Horn Toad were some of his best.

Many say that Midnight was the greatest bucking horse of all time. From the time Jim McNabb of Fort MacLeod, Alberta, first entered midnight in the Calgary Stampede in 1924, he was destined for fame. In Calgary, Winnipeg, Toronto, London, New York, Cheyenne, and other large cities, he bucked off all comers. Only a few men ever rode him. The greatest of these bronc riders was Pete Knight of Cross-field, Alberta. Pete drew this great bucking horse in Toronto in 1926 and rode him to the whistle – the first time this had ever been done. When midnight was sold to McCarty and Elliott and was shipped to the United States it was a toss-up between Five Minutes to Midnight, Easy Money, or Slim Sweden as to which would fill Midnight's horse-shoes. Slim Sweden, up to that time, had remained unridden, and it was an exciting time in 1932 when once again the greatest bronc rider of them all drew an unrideable horse. Pete Knight had drawn Slim Sweden in the finals in Calgary. This was to be the ride of the year, but just before Pete made his ride, a mountain shower came up which drove all folks out of the bleachers to seek shelter and the rain turned the arena into a batter of mud.

When some Slim Sweden came out of the chute, he started his powerful drive that had unseated so many bronc riders in the past, but the slick mud gave way under his straining drive and he fell heavily to the ground. Pete was given a re-ride on the same horse, but the same thing happened – Slim Sweden fell a second time. This was his undo-ing. For several rodeos after that he simply refused to buck. Knight wisely retired him for the balance of the season. When spring arrived in 1933, Lyle was again employed at the Knight Ranch. Knight had his bucking string in the corral and Slim Sweden was in great shape.

9

He had wintered well and showed signs of a promising summer. "I want you to throw a saddle on Slim Sweden, Lyle" said Knight "I can't wait to see if he is going to fire."

My brother did as he was instructed. Slim Sweden was back to his old form – but Lyle rode him. At the Dominion Day Celebration [July 1st] at Raymond, that year, Lyle signed up in the bronc riding event because he was now traveling with Ray Knight's bucking string.

Everyone was anxious as it was announced that Slim Sweden was going to contest once again. The man who drew him came out on him making a good ride till Slim Sweden turned on. He almost bucked his rider off when all of a sudden, with victory in right in his grasp, he quit cold. Ray Knight shook his head sadly. "That's sure to bad" he said to my bother Mel. "I sure thought the old horse was coming back; out at the ranch that young brother of your's rode the horse this spring, and durn'ed if he didn't give Lyle all he had, that boy sat up there and full stroked him all the way, that kid has makin's of a bronc rider.

At this same rodeo, my brother drew a black mare called Black Beauty. When they came out of the chute, Black Beauty really turned on. This was the final event, and Lyle was making the bronc ride of his life.

"My gosh," exclaimed veteran bronc rider Andy Lund "would yuh looked at that boy paw that ol' mare."

It was the ride of the day. Lyle won the bronc riding while contesting against some of the best bronc riders in the business – he was 18. His next rodeo took him to Cardston the two day show that was a ticket-getter in those days. Jack Galbraith, who ranched just north of Browning, Montana, was furnishing the stock for this show. Jack Galbraith was a horse buyer who often purchased horses from Ray Knight – mostly bucking horses. He'd seen Lyle ride some of Knights best buckers. When it was announced that he had drawn one of Galbraith's top bucking horses, an audible groan went threw the grandstand. Old Surprise had a reputation longer than a brood mare's tail.

As Lyle was tightening down, Herman Linder sauntered up to him. "Lyle," he said, "I've pulled that'll horse in the draw at least five times – I've qualified on him only twice. I think the best way to ride him is to open him up first so yuh don't get-goose-egged, than just coast with him.

Polisher your spur buttons so yuh look good to the judges, but don't try to spur him much."

Up in the grandstand Jack Galbraith was instructing his 17-year-old son. "I want you to go down there an tell that Lybbert boy to set his saddle back just a bit more than one would ordinarily do. I want to see him ride that Surprise. He's a good boy, and a bronc ridden fool. Go tell them that, boy."

When Jack's son delivered the message, he neglected to inform Lyle where the advice was coming from. "Well thanks, son – the boy was a whole year younger than Lyle – I reckon I'm gonna have enough trouble ridin' one end of this ol' pony. I don't want too much of both ends." He thanked the boy anyhow, but he remembered that Herman Linder had just counseled him. Herman was one of the top bronc riders in the world at that time he had won 21 titles in 10 years to prove it. Old Surprises came out of the chute in his most conventional manner. Lyle was putting up his usual good ride. Just two seconds before the ride would be complete, Surprised dropped off his left shoulder; Lyle missed the shoulder with his spur and bucked off.

"That's why they call him Surprise" grinned Herman as Lyle walked back to the chutes. "I could see it coming – I knew exactly when and where."

What could have been an interesting career in bronc riding and rodeo work was interrupted when Lyle signed on with the Canadian Armed Forces. For four years he served in Belgium, England, France, and Germany. At the conclusion of his Army career, he tried his hand at farming. This proved to be un-fruitful so he turned his efforts to police work.

He took a job with the town police force at Cardston, a town that lies on the banks of Lee's Creek. One morning the haze that it hung in their air thickened into rain clouds in the foothills becoming heavier and darker, and the rain that had been intermittent began falling like a heavy veil. It was Lyle's Day off, and he and his son Dean had been joy riding. As they rode past Lyle's home they learned that it had been announced that Lee Creek was rising and that a heavy crest was building up in the foothills further west, Lyle suddenly remembered a feedlot full of live cattle, down below the town. It was

11

a feedlot right next to Lee's Creek and was directly in the path of the coming flood. He and his son decided to ride their horses the 2 miles to the feedlot and open the gates so the cattle could be free to seek higher ground.

The people on the lower flats were evacuating to higher ground and ranches to the west had sent reports by telephone that the crest was the worst ever, and that heavy rain was still falling. Lyle and his son began to hurry passing pedestrians informed them that the floodwaters were almost upon them. They knew that the owners of the feedlot were in Lethbridge 50 miles away.

By the time they reach the cattle, water was already running swiftly across the road and building rapidly in volume. Uprooted trees and debris made it difficult for the horses. Lyle was riding a registered pure bred mare that had recently been bred to a valued stud.

He had just turned down $1,000 for the mare. They tore down a section of the corral and the terrified cattle fled to the safety of higher ground. Lyle and his son then turn their horses back the way they had come. The water was rising rapidly now. As they moved along, the mare my brother was riding, stepped off the end of a covert, while trying to keep her footing in the swirling waters. She took one surprised gasp and filled her lungs with water. My brother was swept off of the mare as she went under. He was washed against the trunk of a small tree where he held on briefly.

As he clung to the precarious perch, he noticed that Dean was riding frantically for help. Suddenly a large section of the corral came floating down stream, toward Lyle, one end of that wooden fence clung to the tree he was holding onto and the other of the fence swung around and lodged against a small boathouse that had floated down stream ahead of everything else. Lyle was quick to take advantage of this wooden floating sidewalk so he literally walked to the boathouse. No sooner had he reached the security of that building when a huge wave of water pushed the wooden fence sidewalk on down stream. Also gone was the tree he had just walked away from.

By now, TV and radio crews from Lethbridge had arrived; they began a blow-by-blow description of Lyle's activities in his fight life. A small group of Mounties tried to reach him in a row boat but they.

12

had to turn back because of the floating debris. They tried a second time, this time Lyle's son Dean was walking chest deep in the water ahead of the row boat and two Mounties, Dean had a rope tied around his chest just in case the water got the best of him. About a half hour later a group of men from Cardston who had a powerboat rushed onto that raging water and rescued Lyle Lybbert.

This was the same storm that piled up such devastation in northern Montana. Especially Birch Creek and the Two Medicine River it was said they were running 20 feet above normal and then they converged into the Marias River. Huge steel bridges were torn from their foundations and toppled into a twisted mess as the rushing waters slammed into them. The manager of KSEN radio in Shelby, Montana took his private plane up to view the floods and to give a running commentary of its progress over his radio. A dam had burst North of Shelby, Montana and had swept down into the town, filling basements and washing out bridges and forcing people to higher ground.

At the confluence of the Birch Creek, Two Medicine, and the Marias River, the man in the airplane noticed about 20 head of horses grazing on the River bottom. He could see from the vantage point both the horses and the oncoming flood. The pilot swept his plane down to scare the horses, but they began running the opposite direction. Suddenly the floodwaters were upon them, the man in the airplane was horrified as the 20 foot crest came down on that herd of horses. Too late, they had tried out-run the flood, but could not, the man watching helplessly as the rushing waters gulped up the horses much as ravenous sow would have gobbled up a brood of baby chicks.

So Lyle met a much better fate than the horses. Although he has been a horse lover all of his life, my brother has finally settled down to a steady job with the health of animals branch, of the Department of Agriculture. Through the vicissitudes of life, he has managed to come on in pretty good shape. There had been a few times in this ride through life that he might have been forced to pull a little leather to stay up there, but most of the time he had been able to qualify. It has never been his sole desire to be numbered among the champions – he has been, is now, content just to place in the average.

THE GLADIATORS

It was July 1, 1930. Quite a bunch of us stampede nuts, young and not-so-young, had assembled at the fair grounds around nine a.m. to watch Ray Knight and his cowboys cut and corral the bucking horses into assorted groups for the coming rodeo events later that afternoon. I wished I could have been one of the cowboys helping Ray, but I was only twelve years old so I was just a 'wannabe' cowboy on that day.

Rube Snow and Mel Bascom were also there watching the preparations. They were an unlikely pair to be traveling together. Rube ('Puddin' Foot' to his friends), stood six feet tall and tipped the scale at about 230 pounds. Mel ('Highpockets'), stood about five feet five inches, and soakin' wet wouldn't have weighed more than about 145 pounds. Mel was riding his beautiful and talented horse named Sandy; and Rube was on his big stout sorrel horse named Red.

Rube and Highpockets must have had some pretty bad coughs because they had a bottle of cough medicine there and it seemed to be necessary to take turns sipping this cough medicine every few minutes. Well, as with all cowmen, the conversation went from politics to horses and each of these two vowed that they owned and rode the best horses that ever drew breath. A wager was made; a $5 bet in fact; they shook hands to clinch the deal; they each had another shot of that special cough medicine; and so they agreed that this matter be settled 'gladiator style.'

Each mounted cowboy would ride to the opposite ends of the arena, one along the fence on the north side of the arena and one toward the south side— there they would sit with ropes uncoiled and loops made. Then they rode to the middle of the arena, one at each end. After that they'd come at each other full speed. The deal was that the one who could rope the other and pull him off his horse would be the winner. (Just how this would prove who owned the best horse is still a mystery to me.)

Still quite friendly they each had another swig of cough medicine and gave me the bottle to hold. I asked if I could have a taste, but they said, "No." I was too young to know how it worked and besides my cough wasn't bad enough.

As agreed each took his place at opposite ends of the arena and when someone gave the signal they each let out an Apache war-cry,

14

spurred their horses, and with loops a-swingin' and dust a-flyin', and with the mighty thunder of galloping hooves, they came at each other.

Let the good times roll! ! !

The Gladiators. Western Gladiators.

As they passed each other in mid-arena they each threw their loops at each other's head. Rube didn't catch anything. Oh, he gave a low-flying seagull a bit of a scare, but the seagull really didn't have much to worry about. It takes an awfully good cowboy to rope a seagull.

Highpockets had a little better luck. In fact, in Rube's opinion, far too much luck. Without even dislodging Rube's hat, the loop sailed over his head and snared Rube right around the neck.

Lots of things all began to happen at once. The rope tightened on Rube's neck. Rube tried desperately to stop his horse. (You can see why this would have been important to Rube.) He pulled on the reins too hard. His horse reared up and stood straight up on his hind legs; luckily the bridle reins broke just in time or that big sorrel horse would have come right over backwards on him. Anyway Rube fell off. Actually he was jerked off. Quickly Highpockets jumped off his horse and ran back and loosened the rope from around Rube's neck—for which Rube was grateful.

We all ran out there to examine the beautiful amber rope burn around Rube's neck. Someone asked Rube if he could wiggle his head. Rube did and it seemed to be working okay. Highpockets told him how sorry he was that he didn't miss with his rope. He told Rube that he could keep the $5, and "Did Rube want another shot of cough medicine?"

They instructed me to go up to Golden and Eunice Snow's home (his brother - my sister) to get some iodine and I was told not to tell them whom it was for, and not to tell Golden about the cough medicine.

By the time I got back, they were both up on their feet laughing and joking a bit. Rube had a red bandana around his neck, and now they said they didn't need the iodine. (Maybe they poured cough medicine on the wound.) Things were pretty well the same as they had been before except Rube seemed to be a couple of inches taller than he had been earlier in the day.

Mamas, don't let your babies grow up to be cowboys. . . . They play pretty rough sometimes.

15

HOW TO GET ALONG WITH YOUR BOSS

The summer I was 16, Ray Knight hired me to work on his ranch. I felt he had made an excellent choice. I had broken a few horses for him the previous winter at his corrals in town and in my opinion I had developed into one of the finest bronc riders in the West. And I would go into great detail regarding my abilities at the slightest hint.

I guess the other hands of the ranch got a little sick of it and after a while and they decided to teach me a few of the facts of life. Consequently, whenever we went out to gather horses they would select my amount with great care - some sour semi-outlaw, six or seven years old, that hadn't been ridden in a year or so.

I was quick to discover that there was quite a difference between such a horse and a two or three-year-old green colt. Those old ponies knew a whole hatful of tricks that I hadn't even heard of. If they didn't buck me off, they would fall down, or jerk away from me when I got off to open a gate and leave me on foot way out in the middle of nowhere.

The other hands were very considerate, however. "Never mind, kid, you mosey on home, will bring you horse in with the herd."

16

"Yea, kid, it's only an 8 mile walk, if you hurry you should be there by suppertime. We'll tell RAY you're coming." Or else my horse would blow up and bucked my bridle off, or I would try to hard to pull his head up and break the reins and leave him free as a bird. Here again my friends showed their true worth.

"Don't worry about a thing, kid, we will just haze you in with the rest of the herd ... you don't have to do a thing ... just relax and enjoy the scenery."

It wasn't too bad unless we had company. A strange car at the corrals would indicate either a horse buyer or other guests which could include (shudder girls!!) who might be watching us; so if there was a car in the yard, I would pull my hat out from all the front of my shirt, beat it into a semblance of its former self, and place it on my head at a rackish angle. As we neared the corrals, I would wave my hand and shout, "Heeyaw, Heeyaw" at the horses so that anyone watching might think that I indeed was performing some essential, but dangerous task, precisely there in the middle of the herd. I would imagine they were saying: "Look at that one brave feller right there in the middle of that wild Bunch of horses, while those other cowards are cringing back, hanging safely at the outer edges."

Only it usually turned out that there were no movie starlets there at all, just some old tobacco chewing horse buyer who had probably lived through the same experience and who I never fooled a bit. He'd say something like: "If you get rid of that city dud earloop bridle, young fella, and get one with a throatlatch, your pony couldn't buck it off so easy." And I'd blush because he caught on so easy and I'd resolve that I wouldn't lose my bridle again if I had to tie it on with binder twine.

Well, between the horse buyers and the older hands softening a bit and from what I learned the hard way, I began to have a little better luck and every once in a while I would come in the same way I went out; just like an ordinary ranch hand. Things were looking up!

Then I had another little stretch of bad luck. I started getting fired.

Ray and I went down to the farm camp one evening after supper to fix Louie's disc. Ray was pounding away at a broken bolt with a big hammer. He missed the bolt on one swing and whomped himself on the kneecap. He dropped the hammer and started to do a rain dance around the disc; I hadn't realized it was that dry.

He was doing quite well on the incantations too, and if his good leg and held out for a few more laps we would've had a cloudburst. (as it was, all we got was a dust storm and a little lightning).

On the third lap, thinking to cheer him up, I told them that if he were to lose his puny little old $28 million he could still make a pretty good living as a ballet dancer in Paris. On the fourth lap, he fired me.

19

I hung around Chance's Pool Hall for a few days, then Ray finally cooled off a little and said he could use me for a few days. I could use him, to, as I was down to my last .60 cents.

Earlier that summer, while walking back from one of my one-way rides, I spotted a herd of deer, so when Ray said he had a hunger for venison, I told you I knew were some could be found. He said that he and I would go out in his sorry three doored car and get one.

I'll bet that poor car sure was glad when Ray traded it off. One of the Cowboys had backed out of the garage with the driver's door still open and ripped it off. (No not me, smarty, it happened while I was still fired.) Anyway, I was to go along on the deer hunt and hold the rifle and show Ray where to go. He thought that over for a minute and said maybe Jake, my older brother, should come along to hold the rifle and I could just sit in the back and tell them where the deer were. We hadn't gone far when Ray ran over one end of a post, a post that had fallen off of the fencing wagon. The post had been resting with that one end stealthy concealed and hanging over a large badger hole.

As he drove over that hidden end the post jumped up. It would've made a nasty dent in the left front door of the car, only the door wasn't there -- just Ray's head.

It must have hurt pretty bad; he sure did holler. In fact, his shout quite unnerved Jake who shot a hole in the windshield and the tail feathers off of an innocent crow that just happened be flying along minding his own business. The Crow did a wobbly about-face and made an erratic beeline for Florida, even though migration season was still several weeks away. That evening, as I headed my horse toward town, I reflected that it was rather rude to laugh at a person for getting hurt, especially when he was the one who signed your checks.

I had two older brothers working there at the time, both in their 20s, and both top hands. (They were the ones who had been picking my horses for me.) I think they have something to do with me getting hired the next time.

A couple weeks later Ray and I were trimming old Slim Sweden's feet in the bronc stall. Slim Sweden was one of the top horses in Ray's bucking string. We had him blindfolded and had one hind foot tied up, but that didn't stop him from throwing himself over the side of the bronc stall and into the same stall Ray and I were in. Slim Sweden got up on his three good legs and did the only thing he knew how to do - buck, whirl, squeal, and kick.

The stall we were in seemed to be getting a little crowded so I backed into a corner. Ray did too, only he back to the same corner I was in, and while it was comforting to have is 285 pounds between me and Slim Sweden, I wasn't too sold on the way he kept climbing up my insteps and spurring me into the shins ... so I give him a little push. But the kicking end of that old horse was just coming around and after dodging hoofs for a short time, Ray was right back on my toes - so I pushed him again, and again the timing was out, so back he came - talk about bad pennies.

The next time I suffer bravely 'til after the horses hoofs had just gone by, then I pushed again and that time, Ray followed Slim Sweden around like a revolving door and escaped. I fell back into the manger and peeked though a crack 'til Slim Sweden shook his blindfold off and three footed out of there.

I was a little putout that Ray would fire me for that. After all, I had thought of the corner before he did, and if I hadn't kept urging him, he never would've gotten up enough nerve to get out of there. Nevertheless, while I was waiting for Ray to cool off a little so he could come back and hire me, I did some soul-searching.

Things hadn't been going to good. It had gotten to where if it rained too much or stayed dry too long or snowed out of season, Ray would glare at me like it was my fault. I was going to turn over a new leaf - no more smarting off or laughing when I should not. In fact, I was going to become an entirely different cowboy.

I would become known as "Silent Lybbert"; the quiet fellow who never spoke unless spoken to and then only briefly. Yep, things were going to be different.

Well Ray did came and hired me again, just in time to save me from a horrible death of starvation, and I was ready and anxious to show him the new "me". It was two o'clock on a sunny afternoon when I rode my horse into the ranch yard, and it sure seemed nice to be back. I turned my hose loose in a large corral, fed him some hay and was read for an assignment.

I spotted a bunch of mares in the big corral and was about to climb up of on the fence and have a better look - and then I thought of the new me, and I said "No Sir, not so fast." Just as sure as I did, something would happen and I would get blamed.

So in keeping with my new image, I walked carefully up to the board fence and peeked through a knothole. There was a real nice looking pinto mare smelling her way around the corral. She looked like she should be able to run. Just as she got opposite me, I sneezed. It surprised me as much as it did her. I didn't even know I was going to sneeze until I had.

She had probably heard all about the famous horse "Whirlaway" from one of her friends, anyway she tried to mimic him but her footing slipped and she fell on her side right into a feed trough, which in turn collapsed, with an agonizing shriek, it spilling her out on her back into a flock of chickens.

By the time Ray got there, the south end of the corral looked like it had received a surprise visit from Hurricane Hazel, and the Corral was empty, except for a cloud of dust, and a few soaring feathers. The chickens had all gone crazy and the mares were streaming across the meadows heading for the blue hills, the pinto mare well in the lead. I'd been right about one thing she sure could run when she set her mind to it.

"Well, boy, what do you do now?"

I thought of saying "nothing" but there was only Ray and me and a blow fly anywhere within shooting distance and he would know that a blowfly could not have caused all that! Then I considered saying "I sneezed," but I was sure he would never buy that either.

So I cocked my hat down over one eye just as I had seen Gary Cooper do one time in a movie and I said "You wanted to know what I did? I just quit". He looked terribly disappointed. I'll bet he wanted to fire me again.

WHEN GOOD FRIENDS MEET

We were sitting in the shady side of the ranch house at the Knight Ranch on a golden summer evening. We had finished putting up our winter's supply of hay that very day so had knocked off a little early, a few even had a bath and a shave and were now just plain loafing in the shade, at peace with the world. Harry Lee looked up from his whittling and said.

"Looks like we have company." And he pointed his stick to the east where three mounted cowboys were just topping the ridge, one was leading a pack horse piled high with camping equipment.

"They're from the Meek's outfit," I said after studying them for a minute. "It's Tommy Bascombe, my brother Mel and Ol' Roz Lund."

We called Roz "old" because he was young and his real name was Rozilund but even his mother knew better than to call him that! That's how Beaver Murphy got his chipped tooth!

As they rode up we all exchanged, "How'dys" and then they filled us in on what they had been up to. They had, they explained, just got back from the rodeo in Shelby, Montana and boy-o-boy had they had a wonderful time!

When we asked how they had managed to get time off to go rodeoing they became rather vague.

"Well, you see Jim Meeks had mentioned that he would be in Saskatoon, Saskatchewan all this week at a bull sale so they had just... we... got all that there work caught up and had... well, just saddled up and gone..."

At the look of envy on our faces, they all began to talk at once. Roz told how he had been bucked off over the fence and had "Lit right in a girl's lap," he added smugly. It was probably as close as he had been to a girl since he quit fighting with his sister.

Tommy had won $13 in the wild cow milking (and lost ten at poker). Mel had showed three farmers how to tell a horse's age by his teeth and had been awarded the purple thumb. They had entered the wild horse race as a team and would have won if the saddle had not turned just before Roz got the horse over the finish line!

On the way home, after the rodeo was over, they had seen to it that Mel had arm wrestled all comers in every bar and tavern between Shelby, Montana and Warner, Alberta and "Never lost one." They had been arm wrestling for beer which not only explained their jovial mood but also explained how they had overshot their own ranch by 11 miles and ended up at ours.

You may be interested to know that in later years, Mel would become quite depressed because he had never had a chance to twist with Samson or Mammy Yokum. Grandma tried to cheer him up by telling him, "Vell, iff you vould yust mend your vays might be you could ving twist mit dem on der odder side." She must have said the right thing; Mel has been living like a monk ever since just waiting for his chance.

No, they would not stay the night, or even for supper. They did not want to pack and unpack the sullen pinto pack horse.

"He bites," explained Roz.

26

"He really does," agreed Mel and held up his thumb as evidence.

"But before we go," said Tommy, "we want to show you how Roz spurred that bareback bronc down there in Shelby." And so saying, he reached out slowly and carefully took the pack horse by the ears and said, "Get on him Roz."

"OK," said Roz.

"Yea! You just do that little thing, Roz," said the pinto pack horse under his breath. That little pinto recalled as if it was yesterday how he and his little sorrel filly friend had been standing in a shallow pond just stamping and swishing flies. He had just gotten up nerve enough to place his chin on her withers and after a short moment, she had done the same and he had almost swooned with delight. Such a beautiful friendship! It was strictly platonic mind you. Due to an accident in his youth—but it was a beautiful moment just the same and he was just wondering if this was the beginning of true love!

Suddenly over the hill came these three hated cowboys swinging their loops and ki-yi-ing like a Navajo war party. He and his filly had made a run for it but his luck had run out when he ducked hard to the right to miss a swirling loop and ran right into another one. As a result he had been forced to accompany them back to the cow camp where they had loaded him with that despicable pack saddle piled high with camping equipment and groceries and without so much as a "by your leave," he had been forced to trudge all the way down to that place in Montana where all the noise was.

Actually, the stay in Montana had not been too bad after all because there in the livery stable's corral he had met another filly. A cute little black number this time, she had come in after he did so that she never did see him under that degrading pack saddle. He had feigned a limp and managed to convey the impression that he was actually a valuable steer-roping horse who had been wounded by a ferocious bull at the Calgary Stampede.

He had even fought off another gelding who had tried to get smart with her and thus he had won her heart and so they were inseparable for the next three days. Man oh man was he grateful that she had left first so she did not have to see him humiliated once more by those unprincipled cowboys and that stupid pack! But now maybe his time had come! He hooded his eyes to mere slits to hide his elation, ducked his head so Tommy could reach his ears better. . . and there he waited.

"Get on him Roz."

"By all means. . . get on me Roz," whispered the pinto pack horse once again.

Willing hands boosted Roz up on top of the pack where he got both hands under the diamond hitch, with one foot in the fry pan and the other spur hooked in the half full oatmeal sack. Roz nodded his head and Tommy turned the pinto loose. The young cowboy was not doing too badly until the bronc hit the end of his lead rope in mid-air and sort of flipped a U-ee. Roz soared off into space and lit on his nose right in the middle of our newly planted lawn which quite upset our cook/gardener who had learned to swear as well as any cook in the British navy. Such language! I calmed him down somewhat by promising I would come out in the morning and smooth it out with a rake, just as soon as the birds had cleaned up the oatmeal.

With the cook mollified, Tommy took the triumphant horse by the ears again and said, "Get on him Roz."

Roz lit on the graveled driveway that time and lay there for a few moments just enjoying the fireworks. We helped him to his feet and by then Bascombe had the pinto's ears again. The horse had actually walked right up to him and practically placed his ears in Bascombe's hands.

"Get on him Roz."

Now Roz thought the world of Tommy and would have done almost anything the older cowboy had asked. I almost think he would have walked right up to a girl and spoke to her if Bascombe had asked him to. But this nose skinning business was getting a little out of hand. He drew himself up to his full height, looked disdainfully at each of us in turn and cried, "Get on him? Well son-of-a-gun-gosh-to-shoot! My inconsiderate sadistic ex-friends... just give me time to light!"

(Author's note) That is not exactly what Roz cried but it's about as close as I'll ever come and still remain suitable for family reading.

After we had stuck the skin back on Roz' nose with band aids, we pointed out to them the trial they should take to get back to their cow camp and we found out later that when they rode up to the cook shack by the light of the silvery moon, who do you suppose was sitting on the doorstep waiting for them? You guessed it! None other than James E. Meeks himself, manager and half-owner of Meeks Brothers Ranching Company. Yes there he was, the one who was supposed have gone to Saskatoon to a bull sale. Meeks was not smiling..

Well, they were too good at punching cows to fire so to show his displeasure, Jim sent them down to the main ranch to fence the hay stacks with big old wooden planks and they might have been there yet if a strong wind hadn't come up and blew all their fences down so it was back to the cow camp and into Jim's good graces again.

In my opinion though, they should have been humbled a little more because to this day you can't be in a conversation with any one of them for more than 5 minutes than its. . .

"Remember that time when us three guys went down to the rodeo in Shelby, Montana and had all that fun while you guys on the Knight Ranch were busy haying?" I find it plain disgusting.

POOR BUTTERFLY

Back in the '30's when it rained in Western Canada, the farmers prowled around their house like kids out of school, alternating between rubbing their hands gleefully at the window and reading the farm newspaper. The cowboys at the Meeks and the McIntyre Ranches got to lay on their bunks and read Ranch Romances magazines. We at the Knight Ranch gathered horses. At least we did if the owner and boss, Ray, could make it out from town. We doubted if he could make out on a day such as this, not even in his Model A. Still you could never tell about those darned cars, so we kept our ears peeled. The muffler was firmly embedded in the east bank of a buffalo wallow somewhere, out there in the southwest field, so he and that car never sneaked up on anybody.

Our hopes were dashed as we caught the sound of his Ford and in due time, it came panting and steaming into the yard, throwing mud a good 50 feet into the air until it slid to a stop in front of the cookhouse door.

Since I expect a hot denial from the president of Ford Motor Company, I'd better explain about the mud-throwing. This one threw mud, and it was actually the fault of the company, too. If, in those days, they had put the research into automobiles that they do today, they would have installed an extra clutch and brake pedal on the dash of any car sold to a rancher in North America. Every rancher I knew that had a Model A, without exception, when they got in a bind they'd put both feet on the dash, pull back on the steering wheel and holler, "Whoa!" It was in this position that Ray had previously coasted through a cluster of bush and, as a result, the left front fender was missing and the Ford had taken on the appearance of a holy man of India with one headlight gazing perpetually and devoutly into heaven. So you see, it did throw mud!

31

Ray Knight was a cultured man and a world traveler and a collector of rare paintings: his home in town boasted a Rembrandt, two Picassos, and two Van Goughs; he would have papered the walls with Charlie Russell's paintings if his wife had let him. But to him the most beautiful sight this side of heaven was a cowboy so splattered with mud that you had to guess who he was; and the most inspiring music on earth was the splat, splat of the hoofs of 300 horses in a muddy corral. Oh, we would gather horses all right, we knew that; the only thing we didn't know was which field.

We were a sad bunch of cowboys that morning but the saddest of all was Bob LaCrosse. He had just finished polishing his butterfly cowboy boots, the love of his life, which had cost him two month's pay and a 60-mile ride horseback to the Friar Tuck Ranch down in Montana. In those days there was a reciprocal trade agreement between the ranch hands of Southern Alberta and those living in Northern Montana, whereby certain articles of merchandise were allowed to flow across the border duty-free. The principal articles going north were saddles, hats, boots, spurs, and Bull Durham tobacco; those things going south were Norwegian snuff, chokecherry wine, Hudson Bay blankets, and Rogers Golden Syrup in 10-pound tins. Since there was not a customs office for 50 miles in either direction, this was accomplished by simply taking the border fence down wherever they happened to come to, and carefully stapling it back up again after they had crossed over. It was a hands-across-the-border sort of thing, ranch hands no less. With the introduction of radar beams and airborne border patrols, the privilege was discontinued, or withdrawn, or discovered, or something.

So we would gather horses—and Bob had his boots polished and even worse he had no rubber boots. But Andy Noell had rubber boots, just Bob's size, if he could figure how to get to them first. Bob didn't eat much breakfast that morning and when the rest of us got out to the barn he was already saddled, mounted and slickered up—and rubber-booted. As we approached, Bob began a detailed study of the stars. Since it was overcast and raining, this required a great deal of concentration. He was still trying to locate the Big Dipper when the rest of us left the yard. Bob followed about a quarter of a mile behind.

By 2 p.m. we had the horses in the corral and Ray was there to meet us.

"Andy, is that you?" "No, it's me over here."

"Oh, Andy, I'd like you to swing gates this afternoon if you would. The rest of us will stay on our horses and cut the horses into the corrals."

With all the pool halls in Western Canada full of unemployed ranch hands who wanted our jobs, a cowboy usually assured his boss that he would like to do whatever he was asked, but Andy acted like he actually meant it. He piled off his horse into eight inches of mud and swung gates merrily all afternoon. He even sang a few lines of a bawdy song 'til Ray glared at him. Ray didn't care much for bawdy songs.

That night in the bunkhouse, Bob, so filled with remorse that he could no longer contain himself, blurted out, "Gee Andy, I sorta took your rubber boots by mistake this morning, but I sure didn't think you'd have to swing gates in your leather ones. I would have swung gates if you had just asked me to."

In answer, Andy pulled one muddy boot off and tossed it to Bob; perhaps tossed is an understatement since it knocked Bob off his chair. The rest of us hastily entrenched ourselves behind the stove and the beds while Mel, a veteran of many a bunkhouse brawl, quietly laid the table on its side and slid behind it; it looked like a hot time in the bunkhouse tonight. Bob got carefully to his feet, and as he was aiming at Andy's head with the muddy boot in his hand, his eye was drawn to a most heartrending sight. There, gazing at him through the mud, was a forlorn, bedraggled, sad but brave, wounded little butterfly. All the fight went out of Bob.

34

"My boots; my very own boots; my little butterfly boots. All the time I was feeling so darned guilty out there in the corral and you were wearing my special butterfly boots, why you-----!" And then to the complete mortification of all us westerners, Bob said a discouraging word.

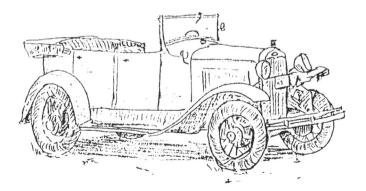

Holy-Man Ford

35

THE NIGHT OF THE COUGAR

Darkness comes early in the winter on the Canadian Prairies and, with darkness, came barn and corral chore time for us on the Knight Ranch. Looking out from the doorway of the big main barn, I could see lanterns bobbing in every direction as my fellow ranch hands, in various corrals, went about the tasks of tucking the ranch in for the night.

As a rule, my lantern would have been bobbing too as I also had my assigned chores. But it just so happened that as I was working with a green colt out in the north field about an hour before sunset, and while riding out there I had seen the Boss, in his battered Ford, as he had headed for town.

Armed with this interesting bit of information, I had returned to the corral at once, turned my horse loose and had already started my chores. In fact mine were done--so, while the rest labored, I watched.

I stood for a while enjoying the scene but it was too cold to stand idle for long. And it was too early to show up at the cook house. Having been told by my mother ten thousand times that "Idle hands are the devil's tools," I began to cast around in my mind for some useful task I could perform all by myself.

Bingo! Just like that, I could see where my duties lay! Doyle Raye was forking hay to the loose horses down by the big hay shed and as he worked, he sang. I use the term sang loosely; it was more like the wail of a lovesick coyote than singing and it was making the horses nervous. Something about having "Incredible tears in his eyes and incredible pain in his heart." I could understand his dilemma. After listening for an incredibly short time, I was becoming afflicted with the same symptoms.

My heart filled with compassion. "How," I asked myself, "Could I drive this terrible pain from my good friend's heart before it broke plumb in two?"; and even more important, "How could I shut him up before those snuffy horses spooked and took out half the south fence?"

"How about scaring the pain away just as you do hiccups?" I asked my subconscious mind (that's the part of my brain that usually gets me in trouble).

"Why not indeed?" answered another part of my mind and I began at once to plan my strategy. Yes, I could sneak into the hay shed by going through the stall normally occupied by those two big chore workhorses—Rock and Snuffy. I knew that the stall was presently empty because I had seen Harry Lee with that team hitched to the bob-sleigh as he scattered hay for the calvy cows down on the east meadow—a task that usually takes a good half hour. (The plot thickens!!) Little did I know that Harry had also seen the Boss head for town and that he too had plans for finishing early.

37

So, I would slip into the hay barn by going through this empty stall. I'd step through the manger and out the feed window there. This would get me within pouncing distance of good old Doyle and I would growl like a bear or something and get rid of all that pain once and for all. I knew the barn so well I even ran in the dark. I was so pleased with my self, I think I was even smiling, so being crouched down like an Apache warrior; I slipped into the stall and had almost reached my destination when I ran my head right in between Old Rock's hind legs. Yep, you guessed it! One of the chore hoses that were supposed to be down on the flat scattering hay!

Rock and Snuffy were tied side by side and had their heads buried in the succulent hay that was in the manger. They were just sort of dreaming of the good old days when WHAM-MO! Some sneaky, creepy creature from outer space attacked Rock from the rear! Rock would have liked very much to have kicked this whatever-it-was that had violated his territory, but it just so happened he did not have a spare foot to kick with. He only had four feet and they were all busy clawing for a toe hold so he could get out of there. He informed his team mate that their lives were in imminent danger by emitting several loud whistles and snorts suggesting that they should evacuate the building at once.

Not being able to go forward they both drew back, they pulled back so hard that they each broke their halter ropes. More snorts, whistles and gasps were immediately heard, from Rock and Snuffy, but more especially from the monster as all three headed for the door.

Now, there are barn doors and there are barn doors. They come in all shapes and sizes. Some you can lead a saddled horse through; some you can drive two horses through side by side at once; and some are somewhere in between - as was the doorway Rock and Snuffy hit simultaneously with one hapless cowboy firmly encased between their rib cages. Luckily the doors themselves were not latched and had been left partly open.

Professor Barry's book, "How to Break and Train Horses," would have tried to discourage doing what we three were about to do, because it just was not possible to do without either damaging the barn door or the horses, but I was not in a position to make any decision and neither horse had read the book, so, of course, we made it. Oh, there were a few broken boards and some squealing, wailing hinges, as well as a dislodged swallow's nest and some rudely awakened pigeons but at least we were now out in the open - which was uppermost in all three minds.

They carried me half way to the water trough before they got brave enough to part, they parted just enough to drop me in a snowdrift on my face. Well, I was looking for excitement and I sure found some. Talk about your fireworks! I'd never seen anything so beautiful in my life! There were shooting stars, rainbows, rockets, space ships, violins, etc. all going round and round in my head for my personal enjoyment and I enjoyed it even more when I was finally able to suck some air back into my lungs and actually get back to breathing.

After my head cleared a bit, I took stock of the situation. All the horses in all the corrals were standing around in tight little groups with their heads held high and eyes blazing, snorting and whistling their terror, ready to head for parts unknown at the slightest sound.

Most evident; the singing had stopped! It was apparent that I had accomplished my designated task after all! But now there was a sort of wail coming from Old Satan's pen down at the far end of the barn. Satan was Ray's prize Brahma Bull, he hated cowboys. . . well, I shouldn't say he hated them. . . actually, he loved them. He just loved to buck and jump right up to a cowboy and play with him. But he played pretty rough so we stayed out of his pen as much as we could. By the time I found my hat and I could walk, well sorta walk. Anyway the moon had come up so I hobbled on down to Satan's pen and looked inside. The Lonesome Serenader with the now-mended heart was sitting straddle of a rafter just above Satan's head calling for help. The playful bull huffed and puffed and bellered just coaxing Doyle to come down and play for a while.

I asked Doyle what he was doing up there in the rafters and he said he had impulsively jumped into Satan's pen when the cougar had attacked the chore horses. Jumping up on the rafters was the second thing he had done on impulse that night.

By the time I had climbed into the manger and snubbed the Brahma with a lariat, the other cowboys carrying lanterns, had converged to where we stood, and were all shouting at once trying to find out what all the commotion was about.

"Cougar!!" said Doyle. "A cougar attacked the chore team!! You heard it, didn't you Loco?"

I assured him that I had indeed heard something that sounded very much like a savage cougar and that I knew that something had surely scared those poor workhorses.

I hated to deceive them but I had long since made up my mind that some of the things that had happened that night would be carried as a secret to my grave. If the truth ever got out, I would have had to change ranches. A guy just could not have lived with those dummies if they ever found out the truth. Besides, in reliving the evening's events, I recalled with pardonable pride that I had indeed sounded remarkably like a wounded cougar just about the time the three of us hit the barn door.

Next morning, right after breakfast, we were all out there looking for the cougar tracks but we did not find any (I personally was not surprised).

41

However, all the hands agreed that anything that could scare that gentle old team of horses so bad that they would refuse to go back anywhere near the barn had to be pretty big and brave and dangerous.

"That's for sure," I said, "And stupid, too."

THE MAN FROM THE PORCUPINE HILLS

A group of us were standing 'round on the street the other day,
When we saw a most unusual sight a heading down our way.
A great big man in a moose-hide coat—he was riding a grizzley bear.
As they lumbered by in a cloud of dust he gave us an icy stare.
And he grinned a grin that was mean as sin, and SPAT—directly at us.
He had a wolverine for a cattle-dog, a live rattle-snake for a whip,
And a sawed-off twelve gauge shot-gun in a holster on his hip.
He tied the bear with a logging chain in front of the Queen's Hotel,
Then he kicked down the door of Roy's Store—Just to rest his legs a spell.
He went into the bar and in a voice both loud and rude
Ordered a double Carbolic Acid—laced with Alberta Crude.
Then he looked around with a fearsome frown, like he just didn't give a hoot.
He looked George Brown right in the eye—And called him a CITY DUDE!!!
George got up-tight, wanted to fight but Walter held him back.
"He's new in town," Walter said to Brown, "We must show him due respect."
"Pray where do you hail from Stranger? And why are you hereabout?"
"I jest rode down from the porcupines. The tough guys chased me out!!"

Grizzly Bear Hunters

In a pioneers cabin out west (so they say)
A great big black (grizzly) bear wandered one day
And seating himself on the hearth he began
To lap the contents of a two-gallon can
Of milk and potatoes, an excellent meal
And then looked about him to see what else he could steal
The Lord of the mansion awoke from his sleep
And hearing a noise he ventured to peak
Just out in the kitchen to see what was there
And was scared to behold a Big Grizzly bear
So he called out loud to his slumbering frough
"There's a bar in the kitchen as big as a cow!"
"A what!?". . . "Well, a bar". . . "Well, murder him then!"
"I will, my brave Betty. . . If you'll first venture in."
So Betty jumped up and poker she seized
While her man shut the door, and against it he squeezed
Then Betty laid onto poor bruin her blows
Now on his forehead and then again on his nose
And her man through the key-hole kept shouting within
"Well done, my brave Betty. . .Now hit him again!"
"Now poke with the poker and poke out his eyes!"
So with rapping and tapping poor Betty alone
At last laid poor grizzly as dead as stone.
Well, as soon as her man saw the bear was no more
He ventured to poke his head just out of the door
Then off to the neighbours he hastened to tell
Of all the strange happenings this morning befell
So he spread the good news both near and afar
How "Me and my Betty just slaughtered a bar'!"
"Ah yes, come and see it. all the neighbours have see'd   it!!"
"Come see what WE did! Me and my Betty, WE did it."

MEMORIES I COULD DO WITHOUT

The Knight Ranch sits on top of the Milk River Ridge on the Canadian side of the Alberta/Montana border. With its ample rainfall and hardy buffalo grass, it's the kind of place that good cows dream of going when they die; and, since it's in the chinook belt, the hills blow clear of snow so there's usually some winter grazing.

However, it can get pretty rough up there in the winter, too. Sometimes for a month or so the snow will lay pretty deep and it seems that the wind will never blow—like the winter that Inj Betts, Johnny Boltus, and I were choring around and breaking a few horses for the Ray Knight.

The snow was about 18 inches deep on the level and we were feeding the few cattle on the place pretty regular (it was mostly a horse ranch in those days.) Anyway we were hauling a load to some calvy cows in the east farm field when Inj and Johnny had a little argument as to who should open the gate.

Inj won, so when Johnny got back on, he climbed on the rear of the load so he wouldn't have to associate with such a pair of poor sports. We found the cows bunched in a coulee out of the cold breeze that was blowing from the north, and as we came up on the north bank of the coulee, Inj said that he had a great idea that would save us a lot of time. I squirmed uneasily. I'd been exposed to a few of his ideas before, so I felt perfectly justified in squirming. Some of his ideas were alright, and some had got me bucked off, stepped on, run over, slapped by girls, and, on one occasion punched in the nose by a light-heavyweight title holder of Southern Alberta.

"What," I asked suspiciously, "do you have in mind?"

"Why not ease down over the bank over there where it's just a mite steeper? We'll pick up what speed we can, and when we get to the cows, we'll just sorta swing around right smartly and switch all the hay off."

His scheme seemed much more rational than his usual ideas. We had a flat rack on our sleigh, both sides and the back were off, and we had a good sturdy front end for each of us to hang on to; so we figured the hay should slide if we could get enough momentum. A second glance at the place we wanted to go down assured me that momentum should present no problem. It would save time, and best of all, some manual labor, to which I was allergic. I got a good grip on the front end rack, nodded my head gamely and we started down.

The speed we attained down that coulee bank was far in excess of our wildest dreams: first, it was steeper than it looked; second, Inj ki-yied, like a blood-thirsty Apache, and scared that poor little team something shameful so that they were running like Man O' War and Sea Biscuit before they ever hit the steep part; and third, when we did hit the steep part, the sleigh surged ahead so that the harness breeching slapped them smartly above the hocks and they really took off.

In the excitement of being on the verge of a great new hay unloading invention, which could, if properly handled, net us millions, we forgot about Johnny on the back of the load. When we got down to the cow herd, we were probably as near as anyone will ever be to breaking the sound barrier with a horse drawn vehicle

The cattle just stood there wondering what that streak was coming down the hill. Inj, like a true test pilot, waited until a collision with an old fat cow seemed inevitable, then he threw a dally, with the right line, around his west elbow, and fell over backwards.

The team came around in a manner that would have made their mothers proud, and a barrel-racing Quarter Horse jealous. The front end of the sleigh was heading north while the back end was still going south. I could see Johnny plainly. He was sitting up now, but he didn't wave or anything; he seemed preoccupied with filling his hands with loose hay. Then the arc was completed and a new invention was launched. So was the hay—so was Johnny.

I have often thought since that we may have easily passed the Russians in the space race if Inj and I had volunteered our services in an advisory capacity around the launching pads at Cape Kennedy.

And as for Johnny, he proved to our complete satisfaction that a person does not need endless hours of instruction to fly. And him without a plane, too!

He flew, with complete abandon, and little regard for his personal safety, under the bellies of 32 cows and a yearling steer—by actual count. Each of them bellered and kicked out viciously, but by the time a cow's foot had cleared the snow, Johnny was four cows away and gaining speed.

In no time at all he reached the area where the cattle had bedded down the night before, and as the piles of frozen cow manure, that he was bulldozing along in front himself, began to have a slowing effect, he eventually stopped and stood up facing us.

He seemed to be a little upset about something and I've always felt that he was going to say a few words. But just as he opened his mouth the cattle remembered somewhere south of us they'd rather be and Johnny was between them and the place of which they had just thought.

We poked around in the snow for quite some time with broken pitchfork handles in the area where we had last seen him, without success. So, as it was getting late, I suggested that we say a few solemn and well-chosen words, maybe even take our caps off in memory of our recently departed friend, and mark the approximate spot of his last resting place with one of the broken pitchforks— before going home to supper. At the word "supper" we noticed the snow start to move a little in a spot a short distance away so we said it a few more times—much louder—and Johnny emerged. He was doing quite a bit of talking but since his mouth was full of snow, we couldn't tell what he said and he must have been a little delirious because he kept repeating the name of some guy who was not even there and of whom we had never heard. As I said, his mouth was full of snow but it sounded like Dan Sonokovitches—probably some Russian fellow he'd worked with on some other ranch.

We got a dandy scatter on the hay. If we could have ever enticed those cows to come back and eat it; they'd have had to lick the hay up off the snow a straw at a time with their tongues.

On the way back to the ranch, Inj and I decided we wouldn't tell Ray about our new invention. We felt that if he knew we were using labor-saving devices he might want to cut our pay, and besides, he might think there was some connection between our experiment and that broken harness tug (now replaced by a halter rope), or the back end of the rack being bashed in a bit or the three broken pitchfork handles.

We asked Johnny how he felt about it. He looked at us like he maybe had something up his sleeve and said that the thought of owning my new silver-mounted spurs and Inj's aluminum grazing bit had driven all memory of anything else from his mind. We said sure,

48

he was welcome to them, and that the reason we'd been so stubborn about selling them to him before was because we were saving them to give to him for his birthday, and didn't it come pretty soon? He said in about three months, but since we wanted him to have them so much, he might as well take them now.

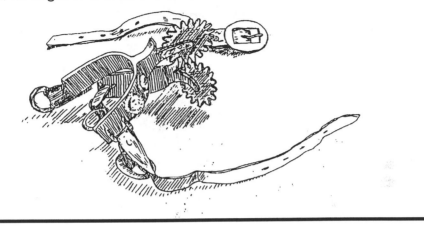

THE SNIPE HUNTERS

Back in the hungry thirties there seemed to be a lot of practical jokers in our part of the country. Actually, I guess there are pranksters everywhere—always were, and always will be. Back in those days we had bad-sounding radio and no TV as a result people found other ways to amuse themselves, so perhaps the practical joker was more visible and more in demand at parties and such; although, we all know they can be a real pain in the neck sometimes, especially if you are the fall-guy.

There were a couple of guys who drifted into the Knight Ranch and stayed through the summer who were pretty high on practical jokes. For those of you who don't know where the Knight Ranch is I'd better tell you. It's sitting right up on top of the Milk River Ridge in Southern Alberta, South of Raymond, Alberta. The south fence is just two townships of wide open prairie—twelve miles as the crow flies from the Alberta/Montana border. One of these newcomers was named Thurston Sand, so he soon got dubbed, 'Sifton' Sand, and later shortened again to just 'Shifty' which seemed to fit his character pretty good. The other one said we could just call him 'Toad Snoad.' So we did. We never did find out what his first name was and nobody really cared anyway. You judge a man by the way he works, not by the name he wears or the color of his skin.

As I said before, they were high on practical jokes and I'll admit I laughed at some of their pranks, but when that cactus was put under – my - saddle and I was soaring along up there in the wild blue yonder above a depraved bronco, my mind was occupied with two thoughts. The thought that was uppermost in my mind was trying to locate a suitable place to land between a rock and a hard place, and thought number two was trying to think up a suitable way to decapitate Toad and Shifty...at least a scare that could be drug out for quite a while, and one where the perpetrator (me) was not apt to get caught.

Well, summer was slipping away fast and there was a chill in the air the evening this particular stranger rode into the yard. He seemed to be a little down on his luck—his outfit showing pretty hefty signs of wear and tear, down-at-the-heel boots, raggedy levis, and he was in a bad need of a haircut and a shave. His old black horse looked like he was honest enough and had given his best, but he was pretty well all tuckered out. Footsore and leg-weary, when this cowboy, who introduced himself as Tex, pulled the saddle off his horse, as he did the old feller winced like he had a sore back as well. The saddle itself was not too much to brag about either—an ancient thing of unknown vintage with binder twine lacing in the off stirrup leather, and stirrups that didn't match—an ox-bow wooden stirrup one on one side and an ugly iron one on the other. We didn't make any comments about his outfit. There were lots of hard-luck cowboys riding the grub-line in those days, and the way things were, it could have happened to any one of us, so we just didn't pass judgment.

He was a friendly visiting sort of guy and when we were settled in the bunkhouse after supper, we visited some more. But it suddenly struck me that though he talked a bit; we still didn't know much about him, like where he was from and where he was going. He told us to call him Tex, but that's about all we knew. He just fielded and side-stepped questions pointed his direction. After we had visited for a while and he got to know our names, he looked at Toad and Shifty and said, "I stayed at Rube Snow's place last night and he said that maybe you guys would show me how to snipe hunt."

Well you should have seen those two guys eyes light up. Snipe hunting was one of their favorite gags. We were a bit surprised that Rube would help them set it up though. Rube was a bachelor rancher who lived eighteen miles north of our ranch. He didn't have too much love for Toad and Shifty. The last time he visited the ranch the had sneaked up on the off side of his horse and gave one heck of a yank on Rube's back cinch, and for a few minutes there the middle-aged rancher did himself proud as a bronc rider. But you could tell as he left the yard that he was not too happy with that pair. Since he had helped to set up the snipe hunt it looked like he might be prepared to forgive and forget.

'Snipe Hunting'—They claimed they had pulled it off several times in Saskatchewan, but so far no one in this country had as yet taken the bait. The thing to do was to get yourself a sucker, usually some town kid or a homestead kid who hadn't been around too much. They would tell him about this mysterious sand snipe—a most elusive bird that most cow-folks didn't even know about because the bird was always hunted at night. The down on this bird's breast was worth twenty dollars an ounce and the average bird would yield and average of six ounces. So you're looking at a harvest of a hundred and twenty dollars a bird, and it was not unusual to catch three or even four birds per night. After the down was plucked off his breast he was just turned loose to grow some more. The down that was plucked was to be sold and the money split three ways amongst Toad, Shifty, and the lucky stranger.

They claimed that they were not all that hard to catch. Toad and Shifty would take Tex out to where the snipes usually hunted. He would be left there with a gunny sack, a lantern, and a pitchfork. They would teach him the mating call of the female sand snipe: "Kaarritchchch-kaarrooo, kaarritchchch-kaarrooo," repeated over and over. Shifty and Toad generously offered to do the most dangerous part, riding back and forth in the dark—back and forth at break-neck speed, looking for the male snipes. When they spotted one, they would haze it towards Tex until the amorous male saw the lantern light and heard the female mating call, "Kaarritchchch-kaarrooo." Well that male snipe was as good as theirs. When he got close enough Tex would just reach out gentle-like with the pitch fork and boost him into the sack, and that was that. The three pardners would be $120 richer. Well, the gag—which every one of you smart Alecs already know—was to get the catcher-with-sack all set up and then leave him out there, 'kaarritchchch-kaarroooing' all night while Shifty and Toad went home to bed.

The stranger-in-our-midst said we could all see that he had come upon hard times and he would go to almost any lengths to come up with a few fast dollars, and he was sure plumb willing to give this project a try, but first he'd have to ask a few favors. The two partners were generous to a fault. Whatever Tex needed they would look after. Nothing was too good for their new business partner. So what was it he needed? Well, that old horse he rode in on was all tuckered out. Fine! He could borrow that long-legged gelding of Shifty's. The horse had been mostly just eating grass and loafing around most of the summer. It would do him good to get used a bit anyway. Anything else? Tex told them he was pretty sore himself from riding that old beat-up saddle he'd been using. Did they think he might borrow another one that was just a bit more comfortable? Sure thing! There's a dozen saddles just sittin' there on that saddle rack, just take your pick. Tex took a long, hard look at Ray's big, black, hand-tooled, silver-mounted roping saddle, but then he just kinda shook his head and reached for a more common saddle that belonged to the ranch.

After he had saddled up Shifty's bay gelding he had another thought. "Doggone it boys, I'm almost too embarrassed to say it, but maybe I'd better call it off after all. These old boots of mine have holes in the bottom and I'm just clumsy enough to step on a cactus out there in the dark; and not only that, I just don't have coats enough to keep me warm out there. I'd just freeze myself plumb to death." No problem! Here's a pair of my boots you can wear. They're my Sunday-go-to-meetin' boots, but one night out there shouldn't hurt 'em. You'll mostly just be standin' around, and here's a nearly-new sheep-skin lined coat belonging to Harry Lee, but he's gone to town for a few days, so he won't be needin' it."

The two pranksters bribed the cook into fixing their new-found partner some cold beef sandwiches, and then took him out five miles south of the ranch buildings and left him in a shallow buffalo wallow, sack in hand, with the lantern lit and the pitch-fork stuck in the ground—handy so he could just reach out and grab it whenever he needed it. And the last thing they heard as they rode back to the ranch was the plaintive cry, 'kaarritchchch-kaarrooo' over and over from their not-so-smart, new-found partner. At the bunkhouse they kept us awake until almost midnight laughing and hooting and hollering to think they had at last found a sucker dumb enough to take the bait.

Next morning they went out bright and early to bring Tex in for breakfast. They had their story all planned: how they had ridden back and forth, back and forth, risking life and limb, but the only kind of luck they had was bad. They had not spotted a male sand snipe anywhere, try as they might. But they were not giving up, no sir, not for one minute. They'd give'er another shot tonight and felt for sure they'd bag something this time.

They never got a chance to talk to Tex; however, because Tex wasn't there. They did find the still-burning, smoked-up lantern, the gunny sack, and the pitch-fork stuck in the ground with a note wrapped and tied around the handle. Shifty squatted down, opened up the note and started to read.

"Good mornin' to my new-found partners and my new-found friends. Sorry I couldn't be here to greet you this mornin', but maybe this here little note will do. I did not see no sand snipes at all last night—nary a one. Even though I stood there for a good ten or fifteen minutes a goin' 'kaarritchchch-kaarrooo' like crazy, nothin' come along. I just never saw no sign of any sand snipes at all. But boys, I'll tell you what I did see! I saw six or seven flocks of Canada geese fly over where I was standing—all spread out in a 'V' formation and flyin' by moonlight, and boys, was that ever a beautiful sight. Just flock after flock—honkin' and a-flyin' in the moonlight—just one of the most purtiest sights you'd ever hope to see. And boys, do you know which way them geese was a-flyin'? South boys; plumb straight South. Every bunch of them just headin' straight south. Headin' right for Texas, and as I stood there a watchin,' I just up and said to myself, 'Tex,' I said, 'Do you suppose those geese are tryin' to tell you somethin'? Do you suppose they are tryin' to tell you that at about this time of year it is a pretty good idea to be leavin' Canada and headin' for Texas? Do you want those partners of your to come out here and discover you are dumber than a Canada goose?'

"Right then I decided that the only smart thing for me to do was to step up onto this new-found, single-footin' horse of mine and follow them geese. And you know partners, there's another reason I felt I should be movin' on. There is a young feller on a long-legged, chestnut horse who has been follerin' me for a spell and I figure he should be ridin' in to your ranch sometime this afternoon. He will be easy to spot. He is wearin' a flat-brimmed, pointy-topped Stetson hat and a pair of city-dude polished boots that reach clear up to his knees. He is even wearin' a neck-tie if you can believe it, fellers. And get this—a bright red jacket—yes sir, a bright red jacket. He sure don't look like no Texas Ranger; I'll tell you that much—more like one of Teddy Roosevelt's Rough Ridin' Crew, and all dolled up like he's goin' to a weddin' to boot.

"But don't let them fancy clothes fool you. That young feller is determined and he's tough, and he's smart and mighty good at follerin' a track—just a little on the young side right now. If he had a year or so more experience under his belt, I wouldn't be headin' south right now; I'd be headin' north, right back to that little town of yours called Claresholm where there are several folks that would want to have a chat with me.

"Purty near had me the night before I rode into your ranch. I rode

54

hell-a-winding into those badlands north and east of the ranch, and he was right on my tail. I could tell there wasn't too much gallop left in that old black horse I was ridin', so when I come to that dry, gravelly creek bed, I eased off north for a bit and then I got off and talked my horse into lyin' down. You boys know what I'm talkin' about—probably done it yourself a few times. You know, when you put your loop on his front foot and pull it up and take a dally on your saddle horn. Then you pull his head around to the right with the off-bridle rein, and at the same time put your foot into the left stirrup and press down gentle-like. Sometimes a horse will fight for a bit before he lays down, but Old Blacky was just too tired to fight. As soon as he figured out what I wanted, he just relaxed and lay right down on his side. I believe he was just plumb happy to stretch out and take the load off his poor, tired, aching feet. I lay down beside him and whispered sweet things in his ear. I kept rubbin' him and strokin' him to keep the flies off and he just lay there half asleep while this here Mountie—I believe that's what you call 'em—thundered past not more than a hundred yards away. If he hadn't been lookin' so hard for tracks, he'd have seen us for sure.

Anyway, I let Blacky lay there and rest for another twenty or thirty minutes, and then I got him up on his feet. I tied onto a blowed-down sapling that was lyin' there and rode out of there the same way I'd rode in—draggin' that sapling behind me. It covered my tracks pretty good. Then I headed straight south and that's how I came up onto your ranch.

"Well now boys, I reckon we should chat a bit about the trades we've been makin' lately. I believe I beat you just a bit on the horse trade. This bay horse of Shifty's is a single-footin' travellin' fool, and if he's the horse I think he is, I should be twelve to fourteen miles into Montana by the time you read this note. But that old black horse I traded you ain't no slouch either. He's a little sore-footed and sore-backed right now, but you turn him out onto some green grass for six weeks or so and I tell you, you will have a horse to be proud of. He's all heart that's for sure. He stayed ahead of that big, grain-fed, Mountie horse for about 100 miles, and I'll tell you that took some doin'. But, and it pains me to have to tell you this, but there's a real possibility that that boy in the red coat might want to borrow a halter and lead that old horse away when he goes—back to that ranch west of Claresholm where he disappeared from about five nights ago.

"Well, if I did beat you on the horse trade, I figure you beat me all hollow on the saddle trade. Anyone can see with one eye closed that the saddle I traded you is a genuine antique saddle, right down to the binder twine lacing in the off stirrup, while this one you traded me is just a plain, run-of-the-mill, nearly new saddle with no antique value hardly at all.

"Well boys, I guess that about winds up this pardnership of ours. The lantern came in handy for writing this note and now the sky is starting to light up in the east, so I best be movin' on. But, boys, I tell you, it's sure been a pleasure knowin' and doin' business with you. If you ever get down Texas way, and if our trails happen to cross—I'll tell you right now fellers—if that happens, you can know this for sure: The drinks are on me! So long for now. Good luck on the snipe huntin'. From your old pardner, Tex.

"P.S. By the way, that Mountie feller will be lookin' for a bad-lookin', bad-actin', hold-up man who was supposed to have took $600 from one of them small grocery stores north of Claresholm. You just tell him that you sure didn't see anyone that looked anything like that—just an old, tough-luck, down-at-the-heel Texas cowboy, who was longin' to be back home. And if he asks you if you saw anything of a money belt with $600 in it, why you can honestly say that you never say anything like that—no sir, not at all. So long pards!"

It was getting towards the end of November when Toad and Shifty left the ranch. It still hadn't snowed much and there was a soft gentle Chinook breeze blowing in from the west—just the right kind of day to be traveling. They were headed west. Said they might look for a ridin' job over there south of Pincher Creek somewhere. It was a little late to be heading out looking for work, the weaning and gathering for market were pretty well finished up. They knew that and they'd have liked to have left sooner, but there were bills that had to be cleared up.

First, they had to work off the price of a nearly-new ranch saddle, and Harry Lee had to be paid for a nearly-new, sheepskin coat. Of course Shifty couldn't leave on foot, so he had to buy a horse from the ranch. He bought a pretty, common-looking gelding that was out of a stubby little work mare and a thoroughbred stud. This horse was not too much to look at—head a little too big, neck a little too short, too much hair on his legs, and he could never make up his mind what color he wanted to be—black like his mother or chestnut like his daddy, so he settled for halfway between.

You know the type—a dark brown on top that faded away to a sandy yellow color on the belly. He was docile enough that he broke out pretty fast and he tried his level best to be a good saddle horse, but try as he might, he just couldn't get the hang of that long, swinging walk that a cowboy loves so much. He tried, but about all he could accomplish was to stub his toe every five or six steps. But there was one thing about him that Shifty liked. He was about the cheapest horse on the ranch and cheap was mighty important to Toad and Shifty right now. It meant that they could leave this ranch with its bunch of jeering, teasing, uncouth idiots that worked on this particular ranch and called themselves, 'COWBOYS—about a month sooner than if they had bought a better horse.

The last time we saw them, they were headed west and we all stepped out on the porch to bid them good-bye. They answered by giving us some rude and crude suggestions, but we being a bunch of well-brought-up-boy scout types of turn-the-other-checkers, merely smiled and waved and wished them good luck on their snipe hunting expeditions and someone hoped out loud that Shifty's horse didn't fall down too often.

I should add that they left with grins on their faces. They knew they had been bested and were glad to see the last of us for a while. But there was no animosity between us. If one of us got into a tussle with some of oil-field rough-necks (they're tough little rascals you know.) If we were doing the Texas two-step and were short a partner, they would have stepped in and helped as a matter of course. If I got a black eye out of the deal, they'd have been glad about that too.

"Why?" you ask? Well Heavens to Betsy, I don't know why—because cowboys are just sheepherders with their brains knocked out, I guess.

Oh, just a little afterthought, before I quit. I'll bet if Rube Snow ever reads this little story, he won't just sit there and grin. He'll chuckle right out loud.

THE COURSHIP OF BRIDGETTE O'DEE

Lonely Valley School
Warner County, Alberta
October 3, 1932

Dear Mr. Lindstom:
In answer to your letter dated October 2nd, in which you invited me to accompany you to a Hallowe'en party in Milk River, may I inform you that I have already accepted an invitation to this affair from Mr. Paul Higgins who stopped by the school and asked me formally. I do appreciate you thinking of me. Perhaps another time.

Sincerely,
Bridgette O'Dee

Lonely Valley School
Warner County, Alberta
October 10, 1932

Dear Mr. Lindstom:

Mr. Higgins called at the school this afternoon to inform me that, due to circumstances beyond his control, he would be unable to escort me to the Hallowe'en Ball next Friday. He seemed to have met with an accident. One of his eyes was bandaged and his lips were swollen. I felt it would be indiscreet on my part to make enquiries about his health. Perhaps you have heard something?

I am now in a position to accept your kind offer of October 2nd. It does get rather lonely out here and I was so looking forward to visiting with Miss Pentigrast of the Shadey Nook School. However, if you have made other plans, please do not alter them on my account. I do still have my knitting.

Sincerely,
Bridgette O'Dee

59

Lonely Valley School
Warner County, Alberta
November 4, 1932

My Dear Mr. Lindstom:

It would seem, sir, that I owe you an apology regarding that unfortunate incident at the dance. While I cannot condone anyone engaging in fisticuffs under ordinary circumstances, it has been brought to me attention quite forcefully, by the children at school, that when you struck that policeman, it was actually in defence of my reputation; that a lewd remark was made regarding my person and you sprang to my defence. I am indeed grateful, Mr. Lindstom, to have a friend such as you and may I assure you that your confidence in the stability of my character is not misplaced.

I deeply regret my own actions on that night. I did indeed return to the teacherage with Paul Higgins just as I said I would, but may I add that his parents were also in the wagon the whole time and Mr. Higgins' behavior was beyond reproach. I do hope you did not catch cold in that horrible place and that you were released in good time the next day. Again, I apologize for my actions and hope that you can find it in your heart to forgive me and come see me real soon. Please?

Sincerely,
Bridgette O'Dee

Lonely Valley School
Warner County, Alberta
November 10, 1932

Mr. Kenneth Lindstom:
I did enjoy last Friday evening at the teacherage and am grateful that you are no longer angry with me and am happy to know that you enjoyed by chicken noodle soup. You see, a school teacher can do something besides teach school after all.

Mrs. Whitesell invited me to dinner this coming Sunday and I brazenly asked if the invitation could include yourself. Could you pick me up at the teacherage shortly after noon? The horse I rode last time would be fine. He was gentle and well behaved but alert and eager to please as well and seemed to be of sound character. I am becoming accustomed to riding in your western saddles and find riding in the moonlight rather enjoyable—especially with a trusted friend.

   Sincerely,
Bridgette

Lonely Valley School
Warner County, Alberta

November 23, 1932
Dear Kenneth:
I enjoyed the wedding party and dance at the Ross Ranch immensely and thought the young couple looked very happy. I do wish them the very best. You need not apologize for stepping on my foot. . . they were old stockings anyway and I thought you danced rather well, considering you had a cowboy boot on one foot and a house slipper on the other. I hope your foot feels better soon. Perhaps you should refrain from trying to lasso coyotes from the back of a galloping horse—at least until the ice and snow is gone.

We never use nick names in our family but I confess the alias you gave me I find rather pleasing. It makes me feel well. . . quite frivolous!

Affectionately yours,
Bridgette (Chick) O'Dee

Lonely Valley School
Warner County, Alberta
December 10, 1932

Mr. K. D. Lindstrom
  Dear Kenneth:
  Please convey my thanks to your parents for the invitation extended to myself regarding Christmas holidays and tell them I gladly accept the offer. I was dreading the long train trip home. The mountains seen so formidable in winter. We are having our Christmas party at the school on the 23rd and I could come right after that—say 3 o'clock. Perhaps you would consider coming early and being our Santa. You don't have the build for it but we could stuff you with pillows. Oh, but I forgot about your sore knee. Remember, hot packs to relieve the pain and cold packs to keep the swelling down. I consider it foolhardy to ride untamed broncos in winter; however. . . I'll expect you around 3:00 p.m. then, if that's alright. I am looking forward to seeing you.
  Lovingly,   Your Chick O'Dee

Lonely Valley School
    Warner County, Alberta
    January 12, 1933

Dear Ken:
Well, here it is a brand New Year. Just imagine—1933!!! How
time flies! The school children and myself are all settled down to our
regular classroom schedule again after the glorious holidays and I
must confess I was rather reluctant to return to this lonely school
after being treated so royally by your family and yourself throughout
the Christmas holidays. Such good fun! The dances, the parties and
all that food! I think I must have gained ten pounds! How I wished it
would never end. It has ended however and I am sitting here tonight
looking out my window and. . . dare I say it? Yes, I will! I am just
sitting here wishing I could see you riding over the hill. Please don't
think me too brazen, but please do come and see me real soon.
    Lovingly,
    Chick

Lonely Valley School
    Warner County, Alberta
March 15, 1933

Dearest Ken:
I was rather surprised to hear that your folks have purchased a
home in the town of Milk River and are planning on leaving you alone
on the ranch just as soon as they can get moved. I am sorry to hear
of your mother's ill health and I agree she should be much nearer her
doctor under the circumstances.
I am not sure at all how I should react to your invitation to take
over the cooking duties at the ranch. I can't tell whether I am the
recipient of a proposal or a proposition. Present yourself at this
teacherage at once and state your intentions, young man!
    Lovingly yours, Chick

Vernon, British Columbia
June 15, 1933

To: Mr. & Mrs. Russel Higgins & Paul,
Mr. and Mrs. Pierre O'Dee request the pleasure of your company at the wedding of their daughter Bridgette to Mr. Kenneth Lindstrom, son of Mr. and Mrs. Deloss Lindstrom of Milk River, Alberta.

The wedding will take place on July 12, 1933 at the United Church in Vernon, British Columbia at 3:00 p.m. Reception and dance to follow.

Sincerely,
Mr. and Mrs. Pierre O'Dee

Rafter "L" Ranch
Lucky Stike, Alberta

May 23, 1957
Dear Paul and Marie:
We are having a little get together here at the ranch next Friday to celebrate Devon's graduation from Veterinary College. Please try to come. It will be nice to have a doctor around the place—especially at calving time. Oh, by the way, here is one old school marm who voluntarily resigns her position as bovine midwife effective immediately. We are looking forward to seeing you.
Love,
Chick and Ken

THE END

With Love To Ellie Sue

Doomseville, Saskatchewan
Oct. 1, 1992

Dearest Ellie Sue,

Well, Sweetheart, I'll bet you'r mighty surprised to hear from me since I left home 4 months ago saying that you were fat and sloppy and a lousey housekeeper to boot and that I never wanted to see you again but now I hope you realize that I was only joshin' don't you darlin' cause that's the way I josh sometimes but I sure didn't mean it, no sir, not a word of it and I'm sure you are smart enough to know that good ol'Clem would never say a thing like that about that sweet little woman of his'n so I just want you to fergit I ever talked like that to you even when ajokin' so you just pay it no never mind, nosir, darlin', just cross it right out of you mind.

I arrived down here in Doomsevilee about the 4th of September and went right to work shovelin' grain for this big wheat farmer but shovelin' wheat is awful heavy work don't you know sweetheart and me with this bad back and all, you remember how by back used to go out on me around home whenever I tried to help you dig postholes or hoe the garden and such and wellsir, she struck again and I had to quit and he paid me $72.60 for the days I'd worked and I was about to send the whole kit and caboodle to you my sweet little wife but I had to pay for my room here in Doomseville and I'd been chargin' at the Chinaman's for coffee and tabaccy and grub soest when I got all them bills squared up I was down to $32.50 and I was about to send that to you too and then I said to myself. . ."Hang on here Clem, $32.50 just ain't enough to send that dear little woman of your'n." So I decided to git into a poker game and win up to ten times that much, maybe even more and I was agoin' to send it all to you to just do whatever you pleased with it, maybe buy yourself a new dress or something for the kids and maybe you could fix that broke window in the kitchen again and I was agoin' to do all that for you just because, well, just because that's the kind of guy I am.

You've never seen that side of me before but that's just the way I am. Generous to a falt. But that guy I got into the poker game with was an out and out crook, a cheater from the word go and him with

66

that friendly smile and all and I know he was a crook 'cause he took all my money that's what he did, every dang penney of it - plus my pocket watch. Smooth too, real smooth. I tried by best to catch him cheatin' and if I could of caught him I'd have give him what-for, but try as I might, I couldn't catch him cheatin', he was just too smooth. You'll be tickled pink to know that I've quit drinkin. Yessir, quit 'er cold.   Haven't had a drink since that poker game 4 nights ago. Course I ain't had much to eat since then   either because that crooked gambler took all my money but I was plannin' on quitin' drinkin' anyway. I had told myself that I was agoin' to quit drinkin' right after that poker game and sure enough I did. . . I said to myself "Clem" I said, "That little woman of your'n don't cotton too much to you a drinkin', soest you'r agoin' to quit this very night after this here poker game and so I did, Aint had no drink since that night nossir, not one drop.

Well, I suppose you'r a wonderin' what this here letter is all about. so hang onto your hat darlin' 'cause here's the good news. I've decided to take you back. If you aint fainted from joy yet you should go call the kids soest you can all be happy together 'cause their dear old dad is acomin' home!! Yep, I'm acomin' home to be a real dad to my kids and a real husband to my sweet little wife. I plan to take that kids fishin' and show them where to dig fer worms and help them with their addin' and such and I'm agoin' to be there to help my darlin' wife do the chores around the place like hold the goats head while you milk and fetch in bundles and bundles of fire wood, why I'm agoin' to fetch so much firewood that we'll have to build another room on our cabin just to hold all the wood I'm agoin' to fetch in. (Hee hee just a little humor throwed in there) I won't haul in that much wood, not all at once any way but I'll fetch in so much that you and the kids won't ever have to go out in the cold to get firewood, you can just sit there by the fire and do home work and knit and stull like that.

So there you have it. You'r ever lovin' husband is acomin' home jest as fast as that ol' Greyhound bus can bring him and then we will be a real happy family together once more. Oh yes Honey I almost fergot to mention it, I'll need fer you to send me a few dollars for bus fare. The fare from Doomseville to Alkali Flats is $32.90 so if you could maybe send me $38.00 or $39.00 I could have bus fare and maybe buy some coffee and a hamburger along the way. The bus gits into Alkali Flats at 4.25 in the mornin' so if you was to be there to meet me it would sure be nice but if you don't want to drag that purty little body of yours out of bed at that time of night well don't you worry about it for one minute. I'll just point these old wore-out cowboy boots north and will come home and be a real father to my kids and a real husband to the purtiest sweetest little wife in the whole world. Lots of love – Clem.

P.S. Congratulations on winning the Lotto 6/49 grand prize jackpot. $3,647,611.12 or something like that but shucks, who's counting.

(Here is a little quiz) Audience:

Do you think Ellie Sue took Clem back?
Yes?   No?

Do you think she should have taken him back?
Yes?   No?

Would you like to know if Ellie Sue took Clem back?
Yes?   No?

OK! This will help with the answer.

From Mr. Clem Chowder
Gen. Delivery
Doomseville, Sask.
TTX OHO

                                           Mrs. Ellie Sue Chowder
                                           P.O. Box 556 Alkali Flatts
                                           Alberta, T0X 0T0

RETURN   TO   SENDER
RETURN TO SENDER
    Mail cannot be delivered. Addressed has moved
    They left no forwarding address (Signed)
    L. E. Jones, Postmaster

I Was a Hog Rancher For A Couple Of Days

When I'd come in from the Knight Ranch every month or so, I used to go to my sister's place for a bath. It was nice just to lean my socks in the corner and relax in the tab for a while. Sometimes I almost felt like I'd like to bathe every week; but, too much luxury can get you in trouble.

On one of my trips there, my brother in law (whom we will call Golden Glow to protect the innocent) suggested that we go into the hog business together. I was interested. There was a little filly in a neighboring town that had taken my fancy. I could acquire her for $18 (that's six dollars for the license and $12 for the ring) provided I could find a place to keep her. So I married her and we moved out Golden's farm.

My first assignment was to get an old Sow (a mother pig) out from under a straw stack. She had managed to get away and then she had tunneled back into that straw stack and had given birth to a litter of pigs. Eight piglets in fact. Golden couldn't get her to come out, so I was to crawl back in their and get her to come out - big deal. I must've crawled back in her dark cave about 15 feet when I put my hand on one of her piglets, who promptly set out a plea for help. She stood up snarled "Augh, augh, augh" in a rather rude voice, to which I replied "Ooh, ooh, ooh" as we rubbed noses. We didn't rub noses for too long however - no longer than it took me to turn my six-foot-one frame around in her 18 x 18 inch wide tunnel; then I left and she followed.

When she got out into the sunlight, I got a good look at her. She looked like a cross between a Greyhound Dog and an Arkansas Razorback. She'd been away from home for about 10 days and probably hadn't eaten much, if anything, in that time. But she looked like she planned on eating any minute now, so I struggled to my feet and shifted into high gear, the corner of my brain that wasn't busy longing for home reminded me that I still had her squealing piglet in my hand and that if I dropped it, she would probably quit chasing me. But I was using so much energy just put one foot in front of the other such that I didn't have enough strength left to un-crook my fingers.

70

The three strand barbed wire fences didn't slow either one of us down; I'd hurdle them and she'd go under. I headed for the house, planning to go in and slammed the door, but my wife, who was standing on the porch watching, decided she didn't want a pig and an idiot on her clean floors. She went in and shut us both out.

I didn't figure she had bolted the door, but my time schedule was too tight to allow for any knob turning, so I ricocheted off the house and headed for the pig corral. Golden was there, politely holding the gate open (he always was perfect gentleman). I went inside the corral and she followed; Golden slammed the gate shut and I jumped up on the barn, which isn't too much to brag about since it was only about 9 feet high! Once I was safely on top I remembered that I still had that little pig in my hand - who was, incidentally, unharmed aside from being a little airsick.

My brother-in-law was lavish in his praise. Never had he seen a hog corralled so quickly. He suggested that we go back up to the straw stack and get the rest of the piglets, but I was disinclined to return so he and my wife went out and brought them home in a tub.

The next day, we went over to Soso Osaka's place to buy some more weanling pigs. It took Soso and Golden quite a while to agree on a price; since Soso's English was limited and Golden's Japanese was nil. But I had attended a rural school where 11 of the 15 kids enrolled were Japanese and I had picked up a few words.

By listening carefully I was able to determine that Golden wouldn't pay any more than six dollars apiece, while Sosa was holding out for four dollars so I held up five fingers and they both nodded happily and the deal was consummated.

Golden drove the horse drawn wagon into the pig yard and Soso scattered some grain and shouted something in Japanese which must've meant "Sooey, sooey"; which is what Golden or I would have yelled, anyway on queue about 18 sows and something like 180 weanlings appeared out of everywhere and started eating. Soso gave me a sawed-off shovel handle and instructed me to keep the Sows back while they loaded 30 squealing weanlings. I soon made a fantastic discovery.

If a sow is Babe Ruthed halfway between the end of their snout their eyeballs, they immediately loses all interest in any pignappers. By and by the two men took time to look behind themselves, they had noticed that they were no longer having to dodge worried sows anymore. Seventeen sows were now tranquilized and I was hot on the trail of the last one. They both seemed rather startled. Soso said a few phrases that I had not learned at that rural school.

Golden, being a Mormon Bishop, was much more restricted in his speech, confining his remarks to my goodness, merciful heavens, o'shaw, and a couple of words about which I won't mention since it might get him in trouble with church authorities.

72

There I was, a genius born before his time! In fact, my instant hog tranquilizer system has not been fully accepted by the Hog Growers Association even today!

Later that night, by mutual consent, we dissolved our partnership. Golden, and my darling wife, both felt that I would be much happier on a horse ranch. I heartily agreed. I was looking forward with pleasure to the peace and safety of breaking horses. This hog ranching was too rough for me!

The Peace and Safety of Breaking Horses

LOTS OF FUN AT AN AMATEUR RODEO

Rodeo has come along way since this writer hung up his spurs in 1941 and joined the Canadian army. In those days, Cowboys went to rodeos to enjoy themselves, and generally did. There were some pretty good cowboys hang around in those days – in most any town in southern Alberta and Saskatchewan. Rodeos (stampedes in those days) were a rather spontaneous affair. Somebody would say that the so-an-so could out ride so-an-so; there would be money wagered and a rodeo was in the making.

It's nice to see a group of professionals perform in any field, including rodeo; and you'll see near perfection at almost any professional show and yet you'll still go away feeling sort of let down. The clean-cut "businessman on a bronc" appears at your show just long enough to contest in the event or events he is entered, and then he disappears. He's off to the next rodeo via plane or Cadillac; you don't see him again until next year. He doesn't stick around for your dance, or get drunk on the street or anything like that. Today rodeo is big business and he's riding for just one thing – money.

But an amateur rodeo is different. Labor Day (September 1st), I loaded the postwar family in the car and we headed for the amateur rodeo in Raymond, Alberta. I felt I would just about as soon stay home and watch the old, old movie on TV, but I also felt morally obligated to go. My number one son (prewar model, Dean) who was working at that time at Alberta's main boarder crossing port, Coutts, Alberta, was contesting, and since he thinks his old man was one heck of a bronc rider in his day (I told him how good I was, you would want me to lie to my own son, would you?), I felt I should be there to help them set his bronc saddle.

My first impression on arrival was favorable. The High-School-Boy-Turned-Ticket-Taker looked Angel Face and myself and our impressive assortment of offspring over and ask if I thought two dollars was too much. I did not.

I deposited my family in the grandstand and headed for the chutes to see what hellery I could cook up. It seemed good to just wander around shaking hands with my graying, punchy friends, and to talk about how good we used to be – me never forgetting to asked him if the remembered the ride and made on Slim Sweden, back in 1936. It seemed they did not. They were probably drunk that day, like as not and probably some of them were wife beaters too.

I spotted old Dooley Robinson sitting on his little horse Fritz, both of whom had seen better days as a pick-up man and as a horse, but they were there, just like old-times. What boys they couldn't pick up they ran tough the fence, so the knobby-kneed Boy Scouts could haul them back on a stretcher, as Dooley always said, "Either way, they get picked up."

I felt a sudden pang of concern for Dooley's safety. What if, I pondered, Dooley fell off at the far end of the arena? Old Fritz would surely come back to the chutes from force of habit, and Dooley would have to walk back, with him packing all that extra weight, it could be serious! Then happily I arrived at a solution. I would wire at his big old foot to his saddle, so that horse and man were inseparable. Being a man of action, I wasted no more timely meditation but set myself to the task. Dooley was trying, without too much excess, to hold his stomach in a while he made some witty remarks to the blond barrel racer, so was no problem to sneak up on his north side and get on with the job. I'd have made it too, if Cliff Williams (who soaking wet wouldn't weigh much over 285 pounds) hadn't galloped up and bull dogged me.

Riding for Wagered Money

The rodeo itself was a decided success. My son Dean bucked off his saddle bronc, goose-egged on his bareback and leapt clear over his decorating steer. He cleared the steer by a good 18 inches and successfully depositing his ribbon on a sweet clover stock growing alongside of the arena fence; while his hazer, not to be outdone, gallantly spurred his horse and was successful in running over Dean, lengthwise.

Goose Egged on His Bare Back

High Pockets Warford, who in his shirt in many colors, looked like a barber pole with big feet and a hat, was entered in the Wild Cow Milking contest, where the cows are all turned out at the same time and the cowboys are soon in hot pursuit. Each cowboy attempts to rope a cow of his choice and well you know all about wild cow milking anyway. Warford was riding a little Appaloosa that knew all too well what he was in for if he got Dead-Eye Warford within rope throwing distance of that big, fat old cow, he had obviously selected. He (the cowboy) would rope the cow and he (the horse) would get jerked down, that's what. A situation the little pony intended to avoid if at all possible. But Warford had other ideas.

He'd paid good money to enter this event, $.50 as a matter of fact, and he was dead set on getting it back; and besides, his girlfriend was watching. He was not having much success with his spurs; his legs being too long for the girth of the pony, he was just clanging his spurs together underneath the ponies belly; and while it made an awful noise, it wasn't at all painful, so the Appaloosa decided to stick to his original plan, which was to stay a good 40 to 50 yards away from the cow. Finally in desperation, Warford took a wild swing at the horses belly with his rope, but here again he was foiled by his

77

excessive length, his long arm carried the rope beyond belly and flank and deposited it firmly under the Appaloosa's tale.

Appaloosa, quick to take advantage of any favorable situation clattered down until his tail-holding-down-muscle ache, but after all a tired tale muscle isn't near as painful as being dragged around on your side by a waspy old cow! At first Warford couldn't get his rope loose. Warford finally had to get off and hang straight down on the rope, by the time he got his rope back I suspect that cow had found her calf a got herself all sucked out, so even if he had caught her, it would've been a lost effort.

Yes, I like amateur rodeo, it is even better than old, old movies, I guess. We should have more of them, and just as we were leaving I finally found a guy who remembered my ride on old Slim Sweden, my friend Bill Robbson. "Sure I remember that ride; say Lyle could you lend me a couple bucks? Thanks! That was a really good bronc ride; you spurred that old black horse all the way."

"He was a sorrel", I said icily and wished I had my two dollars back.

SADDLE BRONC RIDE

To the gateman I nods,
leans back and grins.
With spurs up front
my ride begins.
Bronc comes out high
with surgin' power,
Then comes down hard
all mean and sour.
This big movin horse
just took all the slack.
With head jerked back
my hat I lack.
I took an average rein
and two fingers over.
But I measured'er wrong
this snake's took more.
So just give 'im his head
kinda pump that shank.
Hey looka here boys
he's right plump rank.
My bright colored chaps
rosined down so's to stick.

Snap and pop with friction
as I spurs a good lick.
I spurs him out tight
to the front and back high:
While this salty's squealin'
like he's tryin' to die.
As he whirls about fast
then sucks back west,
I show those judges
my very best.
A trilling eight seconds
that horns a nice sound.
Pich-Up men come in
and I'm back on the
ground.
A grain-fed bronc
better'n I thought he'd be.
Prob'ly marked good,
well – wait and see.

By   Dean   Lybbert

(Published in Western Horseman Magazine, Sept. 1989)

79

TO FOUR YEAR OLD COWBOYS EVERYWHERE
By Lyle R. Lybbert

Well how'dy Little Pardner, I've been looking for you a spell.
I looked in at the Smiths and the Jones, and the William's place as well.
The shadows are getting longer; we'd better be on our way.
But tell me, before we head for home—Just what did you do today?
You mean to say that this morning, you branded a thousand steers?
And vaccinated, and dehorned and cut little holes in their ears?
Then you and young Harvey Kyler, caught up with the Beeler gang—
And shot it out 'til you'd captured them, and sentenced them all to hang?
Then after you had your siesta you corraled a hundred horses or more—
And halter broke them and rode them, in the back of Stone's Grocery Store?
Well son, I'm just plumb astounded, and proud of you as well.
But I think we had better be heading back for the home corral.
For the sun is sinking fast now, and the breezes are getting cool.
And the other hombres are hungry, having just come from school.
And I imagine you're getting chilly—For I note with a casual glance—
You were riding those sweaty broncs bareback—Or else you have wet your pants.

WELDERS, COAT HANGERS
AND MORMON GRAVY

Some years ago, the Reader's Digest carried an article that was written to warn the population at large about the menace of wire coat hangers. The article pointed out that wire coat hangers, when left to themselves in dark clothes closets, will propagate at an alarming rate and that measures should be taken to halt their irresponsible reproduction before they take over the world.

Well, I am happy to report that we have come up with a solution. Quite by accident I might add—we would not want honorary degrees with worldly acclaim heaped upon our heads for a scientific breakthrough that came about quite by accident and not through years of research. We are much too modest for that.

So, are you ready for this? . . . Buy your son a welder! That is right. You heard me correctly. Buy your son a welder! And what is the connection, you say? Well, you will find out in a moment.

The ad in the American magazine stated that the Handy Dandy Welder would weld, solder and/or braze anything around the house; also that it came in a handy carrying case; plus it could be plugged into any 110-volt outlet; and that it could be had for the paltry sum of twenty-four dollars and ninety-five cents!

After some discussion, Ross drew the required money from his savings account (leaving a balance of .05 cents) and the Handy Dandy Welder was headed for our home. Freight and duty amounted to thirteen dollars and sixty cents which the boy's father dug out of his jeans since he had foolishly agreed to pick it up at the Customs Office.

We unpacked it in the kitchen to admire its beauty. It consisted of what looked like two spools of No. 40 sewing machine thread sturdily fastened in its tin carry case with bees wax and bubble gum.

I handed Ross the cord and said, "Plug 'er in, Ross."

"You have blown a fuse!" said the love of my life (a rather unnecessary observation since the room was in darkness).

"Put another fuse in, Ross, and let's try 'er again."

That time, the electric organ lit up like a 1939 juke box and played one verse and part of the chorus of "Glow Worm" (or was it "The Feet of the Flightle Bum"?) before lapsing into silence . . . and darkness.

"Well, at least it does something," I said.

"It was off key," said Goody-Two-Shoes, "And you've blown another fuse."

"My you're touchy," said the Head-of-the-House, "Have you ever agreed to anything in your life?"

"Well, let's see. I agreed to have your nine children."

"Nine children. . . ha! For the wife of a Mormon Elder, that's peanuts. Why my grandfather had . . . "

"Two wives," she interrupted, "And I had almost as many children as the two of them put together!"

"They were never put together," I retorted, "if it could be avoided." I had her there.

"Fix the welder," said Phillip.

I spotted the trouble. "Here is our problem. I'll fasten these two wires together and then you plug 'er in Ross."

"It's already plugged in," said Ross . . . As calmly as I could, under the circumstances, I asked that the machine be unplugged again at his earliest convenience.

"I am surprised to see you lose your temper like that," said Sweet Face, "And in front of the children, too!"

Phillip gave her a scornful look that seemed to indicate he was already familiar with the word and said, "Fix the welder."

"My goodness," I said to her. "Don't be so negative. If you were an Indian princess, you would be known as 'Princess Rain-in-the-Face'."

"And if you were a Blackfeet Chief, you would be called 'Chief Chinook'."

I stook erect, arms folded, head held high. Sometimes she could be pretty nice.

Ross stood back and gazed at the ceiling as if trying to remember something. "Chinook . . . Indian word . . . English translation . . . 'Hot wind over the hill that never knows when to stop blowing'." The mother of my children nodded and grinned. She could be positive at the most negative times.

At about this time, I suddenly remembered something that I needed to talk over with my brother so I left and, when I returned, Ross had the welder going.

"Look, Dad. I mended the hole in Mom's teflon fry-pan that I burned in it while melting lead."

"Great, son. Let's have a look."

"You will have to come over here," he said, "It's welded to the stove."

None of the welding rods sent with the machine seemed to work so we experimented with whatever we could find and, you've guessed it . . . the thing that worked best was wire coat hangers. We could simply use side cutters and snip off a piece of wire coat hanger and roll it in our home made flux and . . . oh yes, the flux. I didn't tell you about that yet, did I? Flux to the non-welder, is the material used to insulate the welding rod so that only the tip comes in contact with the surface to be welded. Flux also keeps the oxygen from interfering with the molten puddle. It works the same as rubber or plastic insulation on an electric wire, but flux is required to burn away as the rod shortens. Our recipe for flux we found in the attic in grandma's cook book, Mormon gravy . . . consists of rancid lard and stale flour—pan browned over a hot fire. For Mormon gravy, you add water and stir until thick. For our flux, you do not add water. Just roll the rods in it and bake in the oven.

To really enjoy Mormon gravy, you should fast for four days before eating it. It was food such as this that made it easy for my ancestors to fast and pray a great deal. It made a passably good welding flux and gave off a rather pleasant odor while welding but we had to keep them well hidden or our grandchildren would chew on them.

The Handy Dandy Welder has altered our lives in many ways. Wire coat hangers are non-existent around our place. Complete genocide! Our boys are now buying them from their friends and even their mothers are starting to complain. The boys are now taking a greater interest in world affairs. Ross has written to Mr. Suzuki in Japan asking for some bamboo shoots so he can weld plywood and Phillip has a pen pal in Argentine and has asked for some young twigs off of a rubber tree so he can weld new treads on the tires of his jalopy.

Now I am sure that you can see that if you all buy your sons welders, we can indeed stamp out wire coat hangers once and for all. In less than a decade, they will be completely extinct.

So, having made my small contribution to the betterment of the human race, I will bid you goodbye and go carry some water to my cows. We used to just turn them loose and let them wander down to the creek, but you see, the boys have accidentally welded the chain that holds the corral gate shut. I think they are hinting for a cutting torch. Maybe next year. In the meantime, no great gain without some small loss!

EL LOCO BLANCO GRINGO CABALERO

In about 1937 I came out of the chute at the Raymond Stampede on a black bally horse who turned out to be a rearing horse. He never did much with his hind feet, but he'd rear straight up on his hind feet every jump. Rearing horses are easy to ride, and in those days were considered a good draw. They looked like they were hell-on-wheels to ride. The crowd loved them. The judges loved them, and usually they marked you up pretty good just for sitting up there and spurring for eight seconds.

The horses were a bit worrisome to draw, in that they might flip over backward and pin a guy underneath them, but a young dude in his late teens figured he had the reaction time of a young cougar, so if he didn't panic and freeze motionless in a crisis, he'd be okay. He could watch the horse's head. When a horse is falling, he instinctively acts to protect his head, whether out on the open range or—as in this case—in an arena. So you have a split second during a fall to light as safely as you can. Just watch his head. He knows which side he's going to land on and he'll invariably turn his head to the opposite side. So if you throw your weight in the same direction as his head, you will likely end up with nothing but a few bumps and bruises.

Anyway, my horse didn't fall. He just kept on rearing until the whistle blew. Tommy Bascom, the pick-up man, came galloping up there to take me off, and that's when things got a little messed up. Tommy and Elton, his registered-thoroughbred-turned-pick-up horse, got there just at the top of a rear, and my horse came down with both front feet across Elton's neck.

Now, the logical thing to do at a time like that would be to turn Elton sharply left to get out from under those front feet. However another problem had cropping up. The bucking horse's feet are lying over the bridle reins, so the signal that Elton is receiving is not from Tommy, but from my horse. So Elton thinks Tommy is trying to tell him to stay in close. Elton does. There is a stalemate. They can't become untangled until Elton moves away and Elton is waiting for Tommy to tell him to move to the left. Tommy can't get the reins loose to send the signal, and there I am sitting up on top of a horse who is on top of another horse, and that puts me, and keeps me, pretty far from the ground.

85

I just couldn't resist. I spoke down to Tommy like this: "No, no Tommy. You're not supposed to pick up the horse. You're supposed to pick up the cowboy. I'm the cowboy—up here." Well, about that time we came uncoupled; my horse fell down; I eased off to the side and was lucky enough to land on my feet. Tommy just sat there looking at me for a minute, then he gave me that million dollar grin of his and called me a @#$%^&*! you-know-what. I won the day money for that ride.

Westerners

It seems to me the west has built a special kind of man
Who shows up when he's needed most and helps out where he can
He's the guy who shows up at your gate when you're all down with the
flu
You're so sick you think you're gonna die . . . And your wife and young
'uns too
He'll chop the ice so the cows can drink, he'll milk and clean and feed
Then he'll show up at your bedside to see what else you need
His wife is cut from the same good stuff so she's right there with him
too
To mix some bread and boil some beans and maybe iron a thing or two
And even though his own chores are waiting, he'll take the time to stay
To kid you some and tell you jokes and pass the time of day
"We'll be goin' to town tomorrow, so is there anything you'll need
"We'll drop the mail off as we're passin' through and haul another load
of feed."
They're just so dog gone pleasant as they go about your labor
That they almost make you feel like you're doin' them a favor
He isn't much for fancy stuff. Like candle light and kisses
Or slapping backs or holding hands, or flirting with your misses
And his kids say he spends so darn much time, just makin' eyes at their
mother
That he really doesn't have the time to look at any other
Made strong through strife throughout their lives, moving at a hectic
pace
It's easy to see that these fine folks we're talkin' of is our own Dan and
Grace
They have just stayed strong as they moved along, without complaint or
fuss
And we as friends and family want to keep them close to us
> So when they're handin' out homesteads on the other side of time
> A place right next to Dan and Grace would just suit us mighty fine
> P.S. We hope you're going to stick around for quite some time now
> good buddies
> So if we get there before you do we'll sure save you a spot right
> next to ours.

Adios Amigos
Lyle & Donna

Bill Witbeck and His Matching Buckskins

To those who don't already know, Bill Witbeck was Jerry and Monte's dad and Ted and Brownie's uncle. He was a feisty little World War I veteran who would tip the scales at about 125 pounds and stood maybe five feet five inches tall. He was the announcer at the Raymond Stampede for quite a few years and that's when there was a lot more work involved in announcing a rodeo than just talking into a microphone.

I'll tell you more about the announcing later, but right now I want to talk about Bill's horses. He had a matching pair of buckskin geldings and they were both broke to ride and to drive as a team on a buggy. I keep wanting to call them Icelander ponies, but that's not quite right. This breed originated in Norway and had several very distinctive characteristics. All were buckskin in color with white faces and white, hairy legs up to the knees. They had a mane that would not lie down. It just stood straight up, and when it reached a height of four or five inches, it just quit growing. Most buckskin horses have a black strip right down the middle of their backs, and these 'Nordics' did too, but theirs was wider than the others. While the stripe on other buckskins start at the withers and end at the top of the tail, the 'Nordics' (I'm just calling them that for lack of the correct term.) stripe starts right between the ears and goes all the way back to the tail. I have no idea where Bill got them, probably in a horse trade somewhere, but they sure were a classy little team. The most unsightly thing about them was the stand-up mane, but Bill kept it cut off short which made them look much better.

Back to the announcer's job: This was before amplifiers and microphones were even invented, so the announcer, Bill, would gallop around the arena on one of his buckskins. He had a big blow-horn about two and a half feet long in his hands, cone-shaped with a handle to hold onto and a place at the small end to shout into. He would gallop along, horn in hand, and about every 50 feet he'd shout to the crowd through the horn. "Andy Lund…coming out of Chute Number four on Dynamite—one of the meanest critters—that ever drew breath— that's the horse, not Andy." Or "Bud Williams out of Chute Number six on a steer…Better luck next time, Bud!" So, before each event, Bill would shout his way around the arena telling the crowd what and who was next, and of course adding a few tidbits to keep things exciting.

At that time (as it is now) the S.P.C.A. was on our tails for not knowing how to treat animals and they were extremely incensed because of the flank strap—the back cinch on the saddle that was pushed back into the flank area for the eight second ride. It not only helped to keep the saddle in place, but it also made the horse buck better.

So Bill, on one of his rounds, made an announcement something like this: "Mel Bascom, coming out of Chute Number eight. Perhaps you may notice the back strap on the saddle which has been place back in the flank area. It has been determined that this strap does not injure, harm or irritate the horse in any way, shape, or form. It is merely put on as a precaution to keep the hay from falling out." Well said, Bill!

Just a word about the S.P.C.A. and the Animal Rights People who have appointed themselves guardians of everything that breathes, big or small. I am not in favor of hurting animals and neither are the guys I ran with or the ranchers and farmers we worked for. However, these self-appointed sheriffs think that everything we do or have done with animals is 'cruel and unusual punishment' and must be forbidden immediately.

A few years ago they were going on about cruelty to bucking horses, so Doc, Darwin Lund, (D.V.M.), put a statement in the paper. He pointed out that there is never a whisper about cruelty to racehorses. Horse racing is the sport of Kings and there are millions and millions of dollars and thousands of might powerful men involved in horse racing. If you were to knock that sport too loudly, you might get your toes stepped on but good.

So Doc Lund gave us a few points to think about: 1) Race horses start racing at two years of age. Most productive years are ages three to six or sometimes even seven. I have never heard of a ten-year-old race horse that is still racing. By age ten or sooner they are all washed up, or crippled, and unless they are lucky enough to be a stud living on a stud farm, or a brood mare; or unless someone will buy them for pleasure riding, they will likely end up at a slaughter plant as dog food.

2) Bucking horses are halter broke at two years, and may be bucked out a time or two with a dummy saddle on them just to see if

they have the athletic ability to be a bucking horse. At age four, they will be taken to just a few rodeos, to acquaint them with the hauling and handling. At age five they are used a little more. By age six they are full-fledged bucking horses. On an average day at a rodeo, a horse will be awakened at day-break for a feed of grain and top-quality hay. By 11 a.m. he will be out in a pen with other horses that will be used on this day. At 1 p.m. he is put into a chute. At 1:30 he is saddled up and ready to go. Eight seconds later he is headed for the unsaddling chute. Two minutes later he is back where the hay and his friends are. And how long can he stand this way of life? Kesler's Three Bars, Hat Rack, and more were retired at age 22, as was the Calgary Stampede's little mare, Wanda Dee. Scores of bucking horses are still going strong at the age of 18. What a difference!

In 1936, on July 1 and 2, they had the regular Raymond Stampede always held at that time of the year. The town of Raymond and District had been stampeding on that day since about 1903, the first stampede (rodeo nowadays), and claimed to be the first stampede in Alberta, or let's make that Canada. Thanks again to good old Ray Knight who sponsored and promoted anything to do with horses. Ray had, by 1936, a great bunch of bucking horses and there was absolutely nothing in the world that he enjoyed more than to see one of his horses buck off a real good cowboy.

There were plenty of good cowboys around on that day: the Lund boys, the Bascom boys, Herman Linder (classed as one of the top ten cowboys in the world), Cecil Bedford (an American cowboy ranked among the top ten also). Cecil was on his way to compete at the Calgary Stampede which came just after the Raymond Stampede. Most of the bronc riders competing at Raymond would also be competing at Calgary. They were, by and large, the top hands in the rodeo arena.

When the dust had cleared at the end of Day One, Cecil Bedford had won first in the day money and what's this??? Some kid, 18 years old had won second. "Who is this kid anyway?" someone asked. "I dunno, he just came into town from the Kirkaldy Ranch with the bucking horses.

When the day money rides were over the next day, here was this dumb 18-year-old again. He had won first in the day money. Cecil Bedford won second. The top six or seven bronc riders with the highest scores were then announced for the finals. When the finals were over scores were compared and the winner of the finals was. . . .What's going on here? It's that kid again. Winner of the Raymond Stampede July 1, 1936 was Lyle R. Lybbert. The horse he drew for the finals was a black thoroughbred mare named Black Beauty. Earl Thode drew the same mare in the finals in Calgary and won the North American Bronc Riding Championship on her.

So what happened to this Lybbert kid who showed so much promise as a bronc rider? Well, he got married. He had seen so many cowboys and has-been cowboys trying to make a living and raise a family at the same time. Little kids and a harassed mother sitting in the back seat of an eight-year-old Chevy in a heat factor of about 98 degrees in the shade, the baby's bottle of milk turned to clabber, hubby just got bucked off, all added up to the big decision. No sir, not for me, and not for her. My wife and kids deserved better than that. I sold all my equipment (rodeo that is) and went to work at anything I could get. When a rodeo happened close enough to home that I could get to it and back in a day, I'd borrow Rube Snow's boots, go win a day money, and get back to the labor field again.

Well, I'm not overly pleased with blowing my own horn, but someone said that if you don't even have enough juice in your battery to blow your own horn, then there is something wrong with your get-up-and-go gadget.

Trophy; a One of a Kind Pick-Up Horse

Frank Clawson appeared at my house one frosty morning with a handful of notes. "It's about old trophy" he said. "I like you to do a story about him."

Trophy

I told Frank I would be happy to do so. Trophy was indeed something special, and anyway, I owe Frank for some pretty good times we spent together. We had ridden those great Canadian plains in blizzards and in sunny weather. We have bucked snow banks, shared line camps, and traded insults for longer than I care to mention. At one time, we'd begun so chummy that I agreed to let him marry my niece. Frank lives out in Cardston so if you are out that way, you should stop in and see his nice paint stud and maybe swap yarns, and exchange insults; but remember to keep a big grin on your face. He likes it better that way.

Now were supposed to talk about Trophy but, before we do, we should go back a little further and talk about Centurion who was Trophies sire. Centurion in was a registered thoroughbred and, at one time, showed great promise as a racehorse, but because of his terrible disposition, he was eventually barred from the racetrack for life. So, Ray Knight, manager of the hundred thousand acre Knight ranch, bought him with the understanding that he would be used for breeding purposes only and he ended up as chief sire of the light horses on the Knight ranch. In those days the Knight Ranch was mostly a horse ranch, raising mostly draft horse, with saddle horse next in line. I suppose it was just logical but Ray Knight also had a very good string of bucking horses. A great many of Centurion's colts seemed to inherit three of his traits – they were fast, good-looking, and mean.

The United States cavalry like the kind of colts that Centurion threw and would just about keep the Knight Ranch cleaned out of broke saddle horses. Ray would write to the U.S. cavalry whenever he got 75 or 80 head of green broke, and they would send a buyer up and take most of them. They didn't need to be broke really well, from what we hear, those boys who broke remount horses for the U.S. Army were no slouch's when it came to taking the kinks of a green broke horse, but that's another story.

Trophy's grandmother was a huge draft type mare imported from Europe. Her registered breed was called Suffolk Punch. The filly colt born of that union was bred back to Centurion and as a three old, probably by accident, and she gave birth to Trophy. Lou Brandley bought him as a colt, and by the time he was three old, he had buffaloed all the local cowboys; so Frank traded a white mule for him. Frank claims that trophy was a freak. He stood 18 hands high and weighed 1400 pounds but was so well proportioned that, from a short distance, he didn't look all that big. You had to get right up to him and look way, way up before you were really conscious of its size. He handled himself well, too - quick as a cat, a real athlete. Frank's notes say that Trophy finally quit bucking him off, not because

93

Frank broke him of it, but because it happened so often that the big horse finally got bored and just gave up in disgust.

In 1944, Frank and trophy help trail herd of cattle from down near the U.S. border to some open range of near Brooks, Alberta – a drive of about 195 miles. A cowboy by the name of Jack Hass (this is a fictitious name, there is a silent "H"), told Frank he was babying Trophy too much.

"What he needs" said Jack "is for some one to spurn the buck out of him."

"Be my guest," said Frank

Trophy bucked Jack Hass so high it began to look like he would never land. It did not take the bucked out a Trophy, but it sure took the buck out of Jack. In fact Jack dropped out of the cattle drive as they neared the city of Medicine Hat - pleading a sore neck. We heard later that he sold his saddle and had rented a small vegetable market garden down on the sand flats on the city's outskirts.

Frank rode the big sorrel for three years before they got to where they could tolerate each other and the horse never seemed to enjoy life very much until he started to pick up bronc riders at the small rodeos around their area.

Then in 1946, they were invited to share the pick up duties at the Calgary Stampede. They never missed a performance at that great show until the two of them retired from active rodeo in 1959. Trophy just loved his work, and Frank said the hardest part about all was trying to hold the big gelding back until the whistle blew.

One of Reg Kessler's bucking horses was a big sorrel bronc whose hobby, aside from throwing good Cowboys, was biting pick-up men, or their horses, so most of the pick-up crew hated to see this bronc come out of chute. But not Trophy. He just loved to take him on. Trophy would thundered down the arena – pick-up man and cowboy forgotten – striking, biting, taking any gouging like a pair of range studs. Needless to say Frank was there but he was there just for the ride. Big red was in such a good mood after one of these workouts that he might go 15 to 20 minutes afterwards was what's so much as even trying to step on Frank's toe. Mind you we do need to understand that Frank Clawson was a very good pick-up man.

Frank said that every once in a while, a bronc rider would get off the bronc too quick, and light on the big horse's neck and the forward momentum would slide the rider ahead to where he stripped the bridle off of that wonderful pick-up horse. This seemed to embarrass Trophy who would cost his head, stomp his foot, and snort his displeasure until he was decent again. That is once again wearing his bridle. Frank found a piece of software rope and tied his bridle in place so firmly that it just could not happen again. That's how much respect they had for each other's feelings.

At one rodeo Frank was riding up to take Don McKay off of a rank old bronc, but Don couldn't wait. Suddenly he was spread eagle at of a height of about 18 feet (or so) and looking forward to a pretty rough landing when Trophy actually changed directions enough to running in between Dawn's legs. One second Don was airborne and the next he was sitting backwards looking directly at Frank. He had landed on Trophy's neck, so close to the saddle he could've leaned slightly forward and kissed Frank. Frank said for a minute there he was afraid Don was going to do just that, which wouldn't have been fair. Trophy was the one who deserve the kiss.

On another occasion, another unfortunate cowboy was bucked off and hung up in one of the stirrups of his bronc saddle. The horse was bucking and running down the fence line, dragging the cowboy and it meant that the cowboy's brains might be bashed out on a post at any time. For a moment, everyone stood paralyzed ... everyone but Trophy.

96

He seemed to size up the situation and decided what had to be done. He lunged forward and wedged the Bronc's head in between his shoulder and a post and then held him there as long as it took Frank to tie the Bronc's halter rope around the post. The bucking horse lurched against the rope and was immediately smothered with cowboys who held him down until the bronc-rider's buddies got him free.

Ken Tail Feathers, from the Blood Indian Reserve, was Frank's pickup partner. Ken is a brother to the late Gerald Tail Feathers, the famed Indian artist who did several of the covers for the Western horsemen magazine and also the Canadian cattlemen magazine before his untimely death. Anyway after many of the rodeos, Ken would take off his shirt and boots, stick a feather or two in his hair and win the partners a little extra money in the Indian free-for-all using Trophy as a racehorse.

One year Frank had contracted the pickup duties at the Brooks Alberta rodeo, but just a couple days before the rodeo he had a horse fall on him and he was injured for a few days and could not perform. So, he sent Trophy and Pat, his 14-year-old son. Quite understandably, the Cowboys were a bit apprehensive about having a 14 year old boy as their pick-upper, but after three or four times, there were no complaints. Pat didn't outstanding job, but he would never take any of the credit.

"Heck," he said "I never did anything. Trophy did all. I just sat up there and make it look respectable."

When trophy he was 23 years old, Murray Clarke (who lives in northern Alberta, near Clarkson) decided it was time for the big old sorrow to retire so he told Frank he'd better give him a horse. "I have a little pasture just down below my house with a nice little creek running through it and some evergreen trees for shade. There is a bummer calf, a one eyed cow, a goat, and a couple of horses in there, but they fight a lot. They need someone who can keep them in line. I won't ride him hardly at all; just once in a while when I have nothing else to do."

It was a tough decision for Frank, but he knew he had to let his horse go. He is sure he earned a little bit of retirement. But, there was a tear in Frank's eye as he saw his pal being trailered away for the last time.

A couple of years later, Frank and Murray had a chance to meet at the Pallister Hotel in Calgary.

"High Murray, glad to see you! How is my old buddy Trophy getting along?"

"How are you, Frank? Trophies just fine! He is the boss horse up there. I don't ride him anymore because the last time he did he bucked me off!"

It seemed that Murray's neighbor phoned one day and said that he had been riding a bronc in his corral for a time or two, but today he would like to take him outside into a near by field, and he wondered would Murray like to saddle Trophy and come over just for a while to act as a steadying influence? All went well until a brush rabbit jumped up and spooked the horse, who promptly bucked off his rider; and Trophy, not to be outdone, up and bucked Murray off just for the heck of it!!

Trophy died in 1965. Frank said he could never figure out for sure just where his big old buddy would end up, with the good guys or with the bad guys. But wherever trophy was, Frank wanted to be there too. He said he wouldn't feel easy if someone else was riding the king of horses over there, and he sure would not be happier riding anything else. It may sound like a mean thing to say, but I kind of hope old Trophy is there where the bad guys go. I'd sure hate to see Frank disappointed.

I'M GRINNING FRANK!!

Ray Knight

So the following is my contribution to the Ray Knight Story.

Ray Knight—Pioneer, Rancher, Philanthropist
Where shall I begin? Back in Utah, I guess. How did Ray Knight's dad, Jesse Knight, make all his money, and why? He ended up with money enough to help the poor and the down-trodden, the country, and the Church. This story has been alluded to before, but those reports were quite often pretty vague about how he made his fortune. It was just acknowledged that he had made it 'in the mining industry.'

The following is as I remember it from Ray's own mouth as we sat around the supper table.

It began down in Payson, Utah in the late 1800s. Ray's dad, Jesse Knight, was living on a sorry little starve-to-death farm near Payson barely scratching out a living. After a meager harvest, Jesse took a team of horses and a wagon and went back into the mountains to gather some firewood for winter.

Once in camp he un-harnessed the horses, fed them, picketed them out for the night, then he ate a cold supper, and then crawled into his bed beneath the wagon. That night he had a strange dream. He dreamed that while he slept his horses had 'pulled up their stakes' literally, and had wandered away. He dreamed that when he found them, they were in a certain box canyon, and that his white mare was standing under a twisted, odd-looking pine tree in a small swale. He dreamed that he grabbed a shovel and dug a hole right where the white mare had been standing—and he struck <u>gold</u>! He woke up the next morning paying no attention to such a silly dream, but his horses were in facr gone! After he had had breakfast, he went looking for the horses, but he couldn't find them.

Finally, the only place for miles around that he had not yet looked was in that box canyon from his stupid dream. He had just plain refused to look there. He wouldn't be taken in by that dream. At last he made himself look there and there they were—the white mare standing under that gnarled, odd-looking tree. Then it dawned on him with full force. The Lord was trying to tell him something.

100

I assume that he got his load of wood home since he was a careful and responsible man. Then he went into Salt Lake City and talked to some business people. They were interested enough to supply him with some limited financial backing. He hired a crew, bought timbers to make a derrick, pulleys, cable, wheel barrows, etc., and they went to digging. He had told his business partners that he didn't think they'd have to go very deep. The dream had seemed to indicate that it was quite near the surface. It wasn't. They ran out of money. He went back to Salt Lake and begged for more money. He got a little more, but soon it too was gone. Then the foreman of the mining crew came to Jesse on a Thursday to tell him they were all quitting. "We haven't been paid in weeks, and we don't think there is any gold down there anyway. So we've got to find something else to do. Sorry about that Jesse."

Jesse replied, "Yes, I am broke, so broke that if you leave now, I couldn't dig up five cents for any of you. But, I'll tell you what, if you'll stay with me until sundown on Saturday, and if we still have not found anything, I will give you all the mining machinery that's here. You could sell that and get a hundred dollars or so for each of you. What do you say?"

They stayed and Ray said that about an hour before sunset on Saturday, they hit the mother lode. He said that they broke into a sort of cave, and that the rich ore was deposited there, so plentiful that it looked almost like wheat in a bin just waiting for them to shovel it into some sacks. So now Jesse Knight was rich and so was Ray and his brothers and sisters. Jesse Knight was able to help many others as well. And he did!

HOW WE FOUGHT WORLD WAR II

THE WAR THAT WAS TO END ALL WARS...HA!!!

I joined the army in December of 1941 and received my honorable discharge on February 2, 1946. I doubt that a more naïve, unsophisticated, militarily ignorant, twenty-two year old farm boy ever existed before or since. Oh, I knew what a rifle was all right. That's the thing we used to plink gophers with down in the horse pasture, only the ones the army gave us were much larger and had a big knife stuck on the barrel, and we were told not to point them at each other. I didn't know much about military vehicles either, but I did know what a tank looked like. If anyone had asked, I could have said, "Oh, yes, I know what a tank is. It's a big tin thing that sits up above the motor on a tractor. You pour gas into it and that's what makes tractors go."

Well, I got through basic training at Currie Barracks in Calgary and a year and a half later, I found myself a Staff Sergeant with the 30th Recce Regiment stationed at Dundurne, Saskatchewan. My Captain told me that I had been appointed to the task of teaching all the men in the unit how to drive, military style. I was given twenty-six, three-ton trucks, thirteen corporals as instructors, one to each two trucks, and about twenty-six student drivers per class. Some of these students were from the slums of Toronto and Windsor and had probably never even been in an automobile before, except for the odd time in the back seat of a taxi—and of course lots of bus riding. I was never given a handbook of instructions or even any verbal instructions, but the officer said, "Train them." So I said, "OK." (That's how non-commissioned officers talk to captains. You'd just say OK or better still, "OK Sir.")

I took my twenty-six trucks, my Jeep, and my boys, and we headed for the hills. The training grounds at Dundurne was a tract of mostly prairie, generously dotted with huge sand-blown craters hollowed out of the sand hills by the wind. There were also bogs and dry ravines and stunted willow trees sprinkled everywhere. The area was probably eighteen miles square.

I'd get in my Jeep, signal to the twenty-six trucks to follow me and we'd head for the hills. I'd head for the roughest area I could find with hills and vales, ravines, and washouts. I'd make a half-mile circle in the snow then tell them all to go 'round and 'round. "And I want to hear those gears grinding. Let's have lots of gear shifting. First you learn how to drive those big, four-speed vehicles while grinding gears—then learn how NOT to grind at a later date." (In those days the transmissions in any trucks were all equipped with 'clash gears.' That's all they had in those days.) I would then drive to the center of the circle, build a big fire out of brush, and try to keep from freezing to death while I stood and listened. The listening didn't last too long. I'd hear the clash of a missed gear at the top of a steep hill and a truck would go plummeting backwards down the sand dunes careening wildly as it bucked over boulders and mowed down a few willow trees. I'd jump in to my Jeep to go survey the damage. Then I'd motion another truck over and tell him to go down and pull the first guy out. Down they'd go. Now they're both stuck. I'd motion another one down. Now all three of them are stuck. But you must remember I still had twenty-three trucks in reserve, and sooner or later we'd all be back on solid ground. The boys now had some wild tales to tell their non-driving, jealous, bunkmates, and they had learned a bit about self-reliance as well.

Since I had no instructions, neither verbal nor written, I just made up the rules to suit myself. I ran that training class all winter without ever seeing a Commissioned Officer come out to see how we were doing. But in thinking back, there had to be officers watching from somewhere, probably with binoculars. I can only assume that these spy officers, when reporting to their commanding officers must have started something like this: "Sir, we have come to the conclusion that if these men can survive the six-week training schedule being put on by this wild and woolly young idiot from the Prairies, that driving in Europe under enemy fire will be duck soup by comparison." By the way, the nickname tacked on me by my Ontario fellow Sergeants was 'Big Bronco Bastard.' But when they called me that, they always had big grins on their faces, so I didn't really mind.

ON THE QUEEN ELIZABETH

We left Dundurne in April of 1943 and after a brief stopover in Borden, Ontario, we were off to Halifax to board the Queen Elizabeth, the huge luxury liner owned by Canard Lines of Britain—the most beautiful and the fastest ship afloat. She was, indeed, a marvel of modern shipbuilding. When we left Halifax, there were 22,000 people aboard—approximately the population of Lethbridge, Alberta at that time.

My regiment, the 30th Recce Regiment, was given the honor (?) and duty of policing "The Queen." We posted a man on every corner between the many barrack rooms and the numerous eating areas on board. Otherwise, so many would have become lost and there would have been bedlam. I was given a crew of three men and was assigned to guard duty manning a 66mm anti-aircraft gun up on the port side of the upper deck. We had a one to three hour stand of duty per day, but that was the 1:00 to 4:00 AM shift. It was a little chilly at that time, even in July, on the North Atlantic; so my men griped a little bit about getting out of their warm beds and going outside. However, it was beautiful out there with icebergs in the distance, the tossing waves and whitecaps tapping against the ship. One morning, about three o'clock, we saw what we thought was a submarine surface about 200 yards from the ship, but before we could get the 66mm anti-aircraft gun pointed and fired, the periscope collapsed, and then we could see that it was not a submarine at all—just a whale surfacing. The collapsed periscope was a collapsing waterspout. I'm sure glad we didn't shoot the little rascal. Had we done so, the ship's Captain would have been cross with my superior, Colonel Warnica, and then Colonel Warnica would have been cross with me—very cross—and if the SPCA had ever got wind of it, they'd be after me yet.

The first night out of Halifax, the Officers and Crew of "The Elizabeth" invited us out onto the open deck for a Welcome-Aboard Party. They told us stories, sang songs, and told jokes. It was a thoroughly enjoyable evening for the 300 or so of us who ventured out to their party. They told of how, as they left England, the Quartermaster Captain made a booboo. (It is the duty of the Quartermaster Captain to see that all the necessities of life are on board at all times.) The booboo made was that a very important item that should have been on board was not there. It was stacked on the dock back in Britain, and they were eight hours out to sea before it was missed. So great was the need for this missing product that someone made up a song about it and they sang it to us. To the tune of "The Ramblin' Wreck from Georgia Tech," fifty voices sang out loud and clear so that all could hear, "Oh they couldn't get the toilet paper on the biggest ship in the world!"

When we were about a day from Greenwich Harbor in Scotland, we passed a couple of downed airmen in a rubber dinghy bobbing along o'er the waves. According to their uniforms, we took them to be either Canadian or British pilots, but we didn't even slow down— just threw them some oilskins of food and water overboard, and then about four hours later, we radioed their position to Air Rescue in Britain. You see, they might have been a decoy to get us to stop so that the German U-Boats could take a shot at us and we couldn't risk the lives of 22,000 men just to save two.

When we docked in Scotland, there were eight gangplanks lowered from ship to dock. With soldiers walking single file down the eight gangplanks, it still took over twenty hours to empty the ship—that's how big it was. Since our regiment was officially the police force during the crossing, we were the last ones to leave. After most of the kit bags had been claimed, we found one from a Manitoba Regiment that was unclaimed. It belonged to a Sergeant, who according to his fellow sergeants was a cruel, sadistic taskmaster. His fellow sergeants figured that the now missing Sergeant had wandered out onto the open deck somewhere in the mid-Atlantic sometime after dark, where he was met by some of his own platoon, and after a brief discussion, they decided that their Sergeant

should swim the rest of the way. He was merely listed as "missing in action," and as far as I know, an inquiry was never ordered. It seems that rules on civvy-street are somewhat different from those in a war zone.

Some of the best fighter pilots were from the Prairies. It seems that when people spend their lives looking for miles across the open plains, they develop a 'distance vision' that is absent from those raised in mountainous or treed areas. Consequently, our young men from the Prairies were much in demand to train as fighter pilots. Not a few, in fact, quite a few fighter pilot aces were born and raised right here in Raymond, Alberta. Some came back with life-time injuries as well as medals. Some, however, paid the supreme price in defending your freedom, and thus they never returned. I am not going to try to name these great fighters from Raymond. I knew most of them but if I name names, I might forget one, and one is too many. However, I might give you just one little clue. One of them shows up at every funeral in Raymond, and he is neither the corpse nor the undertaker.

LIFE IN BRITAIN

By the time my outfit arrived, the 'Battle for Britain' was pretty well over. Thanks to many young, brave pilots and the wily, almost unsinkable fighter plane—the British Spitfire—Germany's attempt to bring Britain to her knees by bombing had to be viewed as a failure, even by Hitler.

One weekend, Sergeant Sam Gerosky, Sergeant Saul Gerosky, and Staff Sergeant Lyle Lybbert went into London. That trio was a rather strange mix for a mad, wild weekend. Two Jews and a Mormon—and I'll wager that some of you may have gone to wilder, more heck-raising parties at a Sunday School picnic.

We were at Trafalgar Square late one Sunday afternoon when we suddenly realized that the last train of the day would leave Euston Station at 10 PM, and we would really have to scramble to be there by then. We knew that if we didn't make that train on time, it would be a long, long walk back to our camp at Woking.

We dashed down into the subway station at Trafalgar Square and were startled to find forty or fifty people jamming the hallway leading to the subway station. We clattered down the stairs toward them, our hobnailed boots on the tile floor made it sound like a platoon of storm troopers. I spoke in the most authoritative voice I could muster, "Make way for a Naval Officer!" Those military-minded British—bless their hearts—parted like the Red Sea, and we marched right through and stepped over the rope at the end just as the underground train hustled into the station. As we were hurrying onto the train, someone behind us shouted, "Hey, you're no Naval Officer!" I turned around, lifted my tunic, and said, "Sure I am. Want to see my naval?" Bless them. They just grinned and waved us on.

Germany's newest weapon after the blitz was the V1 pilot less plane. A little, cheap plane was loaded with explosives and enough gas to fly across the channel to England. It was pointed west and sent on its way. Precision bombing it was not. Once in a while, it might hit a city or a town and wipe out a few blocks of civilization. It was just as apt, however, to land out in a cow pasture somewhere. We used to hear them coming and watch them fly past, sputtering and swaying, and then the motor would run out of gas and they'd fly maybe another half mile before crashing and exploding. Hence, the saying went, "Don't worry about them. If you can hear them, they can't hurt you. It's the silent ones that'll kill you.

Next came the V2, a far more deadly land-to-land rocket. These were launched in France and sent to Britain. They wreaked havoc on a bone-tired, war-ravaged population—so much so that people along the eastern shoreline of England formed peace marches carrying signs that read, "Peace at any price."

LIFE ON THE CONTINENT

Guess where I was at this time. In Southern France stationed just a few miles from where the rockets were fired—miles from where they landed. We were close enough to the launching pads that we could see the vapor trails as they were launched. It was not long before the Canadian Army went in and captured the launching pads closing them down for all time. The Canadians did so after a short, fierce battle with many casualties on both sides. As usual, the US and British Armies took the credit.

My outfit wintered in Brussels, we were billeted out to live in civilian homes for the winter. It sure did beat the heck out of wintering in tents. During Christmas break in 1944, the Germans sent over six fighter bombers and bombed a Canadian Fighter Squadron that was about a quarter of a mile from the home in which I was billeted. Shortly after daylight, Franz Caaboy, my landlord, came rushing into my room and shouted, "Laul! Laul!" (my name I guess) "Come queek da Bosh, da fleer!"

"Go away, Franz!"

"No, no! Come queek! Da Bosh, da fleer!"

I was awake enough by then that I could hear the planes and the bombs and the machine gun fire. There was not a single thing we could do to help the situation, but we could go and watch. So Franz and I did.

After they had completely wiped out seventeen Canadian airplanes that were parked on the runway, they came out over the village of Macklin (which is a suburb of Brussels and also the village in which I was living), and they machine-gunned the streets. Franz and I had only one pilot to contend with so when he was flying west to east, we'd step around the north to south corner and when he changed directions, we did too. I think the thing that sticks out in my mind regarding this raid is that the pilot flew so low down the streets that I could look right into the cockpit of his aircraft. A handsome young pilot—bareheaded, blond, curly haired, calm as the morning breeze—as he passed over our hiding place, he and I looked each other right in the eye. I almost felt like we should wave at each other, but we didn't. That is one image I still carry with me even today and will until I die. That young pilot was the spitting image or Dr. Harlen Taylor. Incidentally, I later found out that all German planes had been shot down and the pilots killed before any of them got back to Germany. Yep, our Doc Taylor look-alike was killed too. Sorry about that folks, but war is war you know.

We stayed in Brussels until April 1945 and were then ordered into Germany through Holland the following day. I was thrilled because my old Sergeant Major was being sent home and I was scheduled to be promoted to take his place. However, I became ill with hepatitis and was flown back to England and hospitalized there. The promotion went out the window. I was in the hospital when VE Day (Victory on Europe) came, and I watched one of the biggest, happiest, most boisterous celebrations in British history—through a hospital window.

My outfit did not arrive in the European theater of war until 1943, and some Canadian servicemen got over there in 1939 and 1940; so naturally, they were given the first boat trips home (including my Sergeant Major), and I had to wait in England for eight months until December 1945 to start for home.

The armed forces do not believe in wasting anything, so they sent me to the Provost Corp Training School and I came out the other end as a Military Policeman. They then shipped me to the No. Four CACRU (Canadian Armed Forces Correction and Rehabilitation Unit), in Reading, England. The Military Prison held all the super bad armed forces criminals from the European theater of war: murderers, extortionists, rapists, and all those who wouldn't change their socks when their feet started to stink. (You believe that, don't you?)

The day I was informed that there was a ship waiting for me, there were four prisoners that escaped from our prison, so pretty well all the guards were interviewed. I went before the brass from the entire army who were still in England. "Yes, gentlemen, I did know that there was an escape from this prison yesterday. No, I did not know any of them. Not only did I not know them, but I didn't even work on their floor, and it did not happen on my shift. In fact, it was my day off, so I was miles away from the prison when it happened. What is more, gentlemen; I have just been informed that my ride home, for which I have been waiting eight months, is in Liverpool. So, whatever you do, gentlemen, please don't involve me in any way with this escape—pause...salute—SIRS!"

I think I took them somewhat by surprise with my boldness. As a rule, non-commissioned officers do most of the listening and very little of the talking, but I think my anxiety and sincerity must have shone through because I was on the train headed for Liverpool the next day.

The getting home was great, but a bit tense as well. In my absence, Dorothy had learned that she could make decisions without me as well as anybody. After four years of giving orders, I was used to people asking, "How high?" on the way up. That didn't seem to influence Dorothy one little bit, nor did it impress Dean, Annette, and Clarke. None of them seemed to even know what "How high?" meant and showed very little interest in learning much about it. However, things gradually ironed out and I mellowed quite a bit. My kids, who had been babies when I left, were now actually people. We soon began to understand one another, and before long we became quite chummy. Dorothy and I had some adjustments to make, but we finally got everything worked out. What do you know? We actually fell in love all over again!

We read somewhere in the Bible that the Lord has instructed us to "multiply and replenish the earth," and it was almost thirty years before we realized that the Lord was talking to all humanity, not just Dorothy and me. We had nine children, six still living—and if the truth were told, we could not afford any of them. We had them anyway. We're not complaining. At last count, we had 101 descendants, and not one of them are doing drugs or alcohol. It's been a rough row to hoe sometimes, but looking back, we don't have anything to complain about.

109

Lest We Forget

By Lyle R. Lybbert

Dear God, if this has got to be
This world of strife, and grave iniquity
If we must fight to save out Native Land
From tyrant powers, and from their crushing hand
So let it be, and may we live and learn
To fight and hate, to scourge and kill and burn
May we not flinch, nor ask the reason why
If our turn has come, if we, have got to die
If this our fate, then we must let it be
'Tis up to you, it is our destiny
But if Thou wilt, dear Lord please let us live
Live to conquer, to win and then forgive
For they, like us were fighting for their land
They had to go at Hitler's cruel command
They had to fight at Hitler's fiendish say-so
Or face the guns of his own cruel Gustapo
Grant us then peace, dear Lord and may we all return
To those we love, to where the home fires burn
May we so live that we shall feel no pain
When we return to those we love again
And so again dear Lord, we ask it yet
Be with us for all times. . .Lest we forget.
Written at 'Canada House' a service club for Canadian Soldiers
in London England on a cloudy, rainy Sunday afternoon,
August 1943.

110

One of My Wonder Filled Days
By Dean Lybbert

Some days we awake full of joyful anticipation and wonder. But some days it is just pure wonder. As I swung out of bed I began to wonder what's going to happen today. Mostly however it gets specific, I wondered if I'm going to get that cultivator ready today so we can work-up the south-west forty? I wondered if that sorrel mare will foal today, I better check! I'm sure we'd all like to have our days turn out to be wonder full [you are right, it should be wonderful] and care free. Well some days can be quite wonderful - especially if you have lots of good help. Number one, a darling wife, one who loves and takes good care of you! Next several grown up sons who are handy and willing to help on the farm. My "some days" really are just ever so right.

My first look out the window assures me that Dale is already working on the cultivator, and there goes Brian to look at the brood mares. Yes and there goes Dan with two milk buckets toward the milking barn, he's even singing as he goes. Yes it is a wonderful day. No, it is obvious that we will not get the south-west forty started today; it rained real hard all night. My, what a beautiful day. I love most days but any day right after a heavy rain is real special. Suddenly I realized that I had before me a day in which I could go see how the beef herd is doing. That herd is enjoying life in a lush pasture north of town some ten miles, yes it rained last night but right now it is nice and sunny and everything smells so fresh, nature in the spring is such a wonderful time to be out and about.

I'll take my old Chevy truck, the one with the flat deck, it won't matter that there is a large wooden box still on the back, its empty now and tied down good, I'll just grab a bite of breakfast and go. I love that old truck, it's a four-wheel drive one ton, with dual tires on the back, me and that truck have been a lot of places together and I know it will serve me well today. I am pleased that my wife made me a sandwich and packed it with a bottle of cold water, just in case I'll be gone a while. My old truck is a bit dirty but that won't matter. It will likely be a whole lot worse before I get back.

I sorta wished I hadn't got so close to the pole corrals and wrecked the rear view mirror on the driver's side, but I still have a rear view mirror over on the right side and that's all I'll need. Windows down, boy just smell the fresh air. To bad I don't have a muffler it would be nice to hear the birds and maybe the truck's radio, oh right the radio doesn't work anymore. Well I likely wouldn't listen very long anyway on a morning like this; besides the radio would need to be too loud in order for me to hear it over the sound of this old mufferless truck.

The trip to the north pasture was very pleasant and everything was quite okay, once I got there, so I just sat and relaxed for a while and then I headed back home. The road up and back to say the least was muddy, with some spots worse than others. The bad spots were a bit of a problem but the truck was in four-wheel drive and all I had to do was gun the engine a little and I zipped right through. It made things a bit noisier but I just kept driving on, once in a while there was a bit of rear end swishing but I got there and now I was on the way back home. What a wonderful day!

Just why he was there I still do not fully understand, but there he was; right in the middle of the road. It was a salesman in a nice new car and as he saw me or more likely heard me drive up behind him; he gingerly got out of his car and half put up his hand, I was going to stop anyway, but yes he did put his hand up. It was a pitiful sight. He really looked out of place. He really was out of place! There he stood, a good looking fellow, blonde hair and well dressed. He was wearing what I would guess was a $500 suit, and a $100 pair of shoes and I'd bet that tie cost $25 at least. Then there was the car; a Cadillac, white of course, but right now a bit muddy.

Here he was out in the boonies and he was in trouble; he had rushed through one deep mud puddle and water had splashed up onto the car's motor and the sparkplugs had got wet. This of course made it so that the motor would no longer run. Boy was he ever glad to see me; he knew he was in trouble. He knew he was where he shouldn't be. I was ah struck; I knew he was where he shouldn't be!

I said "Hi" and walked toward him, he stayed right where he was, he obviously did not want to take even a single step with those expensive shoes. He told me about the deep watery puddle and about trying to start the motor until it sounded like his battery was going to quit; he told me he was concerned about being way out on this lonely road and about not seeing any farms for miles. He was right - the closest farm was a good five miles south, and that farm was back in the brush, off the road, and hard to see. Then the look that was on his face became the words from his mouth for he said, "I'm sure glad to see you".

"Do you suppose you could help get me my car started"? We lifted the hood and after a quick look I told him not likely, the motor was just too wet and besides I didn't have any jumper cables. Turned out neither did he. Then he asked if I could pull him back to town where he could get a mechanic to get his car running again. I asked if he had a tow rope or chain or anything. He said no. Then I told him that I wasn't sure I had a chain or rope either but I would take a look and see. Finally I found a length of chain, it wasn't really long enough, but it was stout. Since it was all I had, he said it would have to do. So after I worked my old Chevy truck around his stalled car I hooked his Cadillac up behind my old 4X4. I totally forgot that my old truck had had its mud flaps torn off years ago. I replaced them once but after they were torn off again; that was it - no more mud flaps. Once the two vehicles were hooked up the chain seemed to be even shorter than I'd thought it would be. But like he had said, it would have to do.

We talked a minute about my pulling his car and I suggested that occasionally he might need to apply his brakes so that his car wouldn't crash into my truck. I told him I was not concerned about the back end of my truck just concerned about the front end of his fancy car. He said he would be careful and so off we went.

My, what a wonder filled day! The sun was still shining and I con-sidered it to be a most beautiful day, I had enjoyed my travels so far and I was sure that my sons would have things going well back at the farm, ah what a wonder filled day. I hadn't driven a quarter of a mile until I totally forgot about the car behind me. No drivers side mirror, I couldn't see out the back window because the large empty wooden box and the right side mirror by now was totally covered with mud. It may have even been a full half a mile but after gunning my noisy truck through several muddy spots, yes, I totally forgot about that white Cadillac and the blonde driver.

On my way home I drove right through town. I had no reason to stop! Oh I waved to a couple of people I knew, but I didn't stop.

113

I detected a puzzled look on some of their faces but I was sure they'd seen my muddy truck before. I didn't stop until I drove into our farm yard two miles south of town. Still pleased with the day I stepped out of my truck intending on going directly to the house. It was then I remembered. There behind my truck was a car, no longer recognizable, no longer white; it didn't even look like a Cadillac! There was so much mud on the roof, windshield and the hood of that car it was totally camouflaged. The weight of the mud caused the front end of the car to sag and the front tires looked as if they were low on air. It was rather sad!

The driver didn't look very happy either. His left arm was hanging out of the driver's side window, he had mud all over his face, and I could no longer see any blonde hair. There was mud and water splattered all over his white shirt, his tie had changed color and mud and water was clinging to the left sleeve of his expensive suit. In fact there was sloppy mud dripping off of the end of his fingers. He looked as if he was going to say something, but first he needed to spit some mud out of his mouth. He looked like he could sure use a drink of clean water. After he got out of the car I almost suspect he would have hit me if he had not been so weighed down and soggy.

Anyway he did begin to talk, well actually he yelled at me! He mentioned that about a quarter of a mile after we headed back south he had detected that I was no longer paying attention to him, the mud started to cover his windshield so he turned on the windshield washer fluid, it didn't help much, in fact it seemed to make things worse. Then he turned his head lights on and off, on and off and then he drove the car from side to side trying to get my attention, that didn't work. He also began to honk his horn, but with the mud was so thick on the hood he suspected the horn was pretty much muffled and then there was the noise of that old Chevy truck to contend with. He rolled the window down and began to shout, but he soon discovered he needed to keep his head inside the car so any shouting was quite useless.

He tried waving his left arm but that also was of no avail. Also he began to slam the car brakes on over and over, but with the road being so muddy the car's tires just skidded along unnoticed and any hopes of breaking that short chain were soon gone. He began to use the brakes rather sparingly because he could smell that they were

114

getting hot. As we continued on, the battery gave out so he could no longer honk the horn nor use the windshield washer. He told us he was glad he had already rolled the power window down. He decided he'd just give up until we got to town. He was plenty steamed by the time we got to town, but after driving right though town he was plum irate. I recall that as he told his side of the story he actually used other words in place of angry, plum irate and steamed.

He went on to say that every moment or so he would stick his head out the window only to get splattered in the face, sometimes it even hurt, but a least he was able to maintain some control. He didn't wear glasses but he did have two pair of sunglasses; he'd got them both covered with mud in an attempt to keep the mud out of his eyes. Gradually he noted that he could pretty much guide his car simply based on looking at the edge of the road and so it was we ended up in our farm yard two miles south of town.

It wasn't long until my boys had gathered around, along with their mother; the boys unhooked his car and soon had a garden hose out and began to clean the mud off his car. My wife helped him take off his suit coat, which he crisply told me cost $800, and it too was then sprayed with the garden hose. In this process he remembered he had other cloths in a suit case in the trunk and by the time his car was clean he was showered and dressed in a second suit he'd brought along. Dale had popped the hood, sprayed the engine and then carefully dried each spark plug and each sparkplug wire. Dan had got some jumper cables and had driven his car up close, they connected everything and it started. I don't think he was anywhere close to happy but by the time he left he was at least sorta laughing about the whole deal with the rest of us. For him to it had also been a wonder filled day!

****

Lloyd Lybbert told me this story in 1963, while he was the foreman of the V Bar V Ranch. That summer I worked for him at the V Bar V ranch. Lloyd told great stories but I remember this one best. It is my writing and not a direct quote. At the time of this wonder filled event Lloyd and his family lived at Cold Lake, Alberta, Canada. This story is about something that Lloyd says actually happened to him and his family. Lloyd Lybbert's father is a brother to my dad's father, my grandfather.

115

Earl W. Bascom - Cowboy Artists

History shows only half a dozen western artists actually live and worked as a cowboy during the open range era of the West - the time when there were no fences and great herds of cattle roamed free. Earl W. Bascom, artist and sculptor, was one of the last living specimens of this rare breed. He had a wide range of western experiences -- rock buster, cowpuncher, trail driver, blacksmith, freighter, stagecoach driver, miner, trapper, wolf hunter, wild horse chaser, and rodeo champion – as time went on he got busily recording his experiences into fine art. Horses were the specialty of Earl's bronze sculptures. He work for the 5H outfit once, where he witnessed 7,000 horses all gathered in one bunch; that string of horses was a mile wide. As he told of that experience he always said he'd never seen a prettier sight in all his life.

Practically born in the saddle, Earl Bascom's life started in a sod-roofed log cabin on the 101 ranch near Vernal, Utah; he was born June 19, 1906. His grandfather had started the 101 ranch in Utah after having crossed the planes in the 1850's as a bull whacker in a Mormon wagon train. Earl's earliest American ancestors reach back to 1630 when his fifth great grandfather landed on the New England shores and became the first sheriff of Northampton, Massachusetts. Another historical relative was George N. Bascom, who became a lieutenant in the U.S. Calvary. He and his troop were the one's who arrested and accused the American Indian Chief, Cochise, of stealing cattle from an Arizona ranch in 1861. Cochise escaped and declared war – this was the beginning of 25 years of Apache wars. Earl's own father was a deputy sheriff of Uintah County, Utah and had the experience of chasing Butch Cassidy and his wild Bunch gang.

In 1912, Earl's mother, Rachel Lybbert Bascom, died of cancer leaving five small children, the youngest nine years nine months old. Deputy Bascom moved his young family by covered wagon and train to Canada to pioneer the newly opened land of Alberta; this was at a time when this land was called the Northwest Territories. The Bascom family settled near the southern Alberta prairie town called Raymond, named after the millionaire rancher, Ray Knight, who started and interestingly enough designed the town. Ray's father had struck one of the richest gold mines in Utah; following the

116

promptings of a dream. Because of Ray Knight the town of Raymond was probably the only Cowtown in the world that is fashioned after Paris, France - all the streets converge to a central point like a wagon wheel, typical of the French capital. It also boasted a fine hotel and an opera house.

Ray Knight had large ranch holdings, the largest being the Kirkaldy or Knight Ranch, nestled in the rolling hills above buffalo grass on the milk River Ridge. The ranch pastured hundreds of horse some 18,000 head of cattle and a large band of sheep. Earl's father worked as a foreman for Ray Knight: Earl and his son John also worked there, Earl notes as a matter of history. Many of the Earl's cowboy experiences took place on the prairie hills of the Knight Ranch.

He remembers when the prairies had just begun to be fenced. One year Ray Knight put in a fence that was 100 miles long – Earl and his brothers and others dug post holes by hand and set cedar poles for miles – they were expected to set 100 posts per man per day-that was considered standard.

Clown and Bull Fighter

Earl recalls that there were two things that Ray Knight loved - horses and rodeos. Ray promoted and supplied the stock for Canada's first rodeo in 1902 and that rodeo (stampede) has been held continuously since then, and is still known as the Raymond Stampede.

It was there in 1918 the Earl entered his first professional rodeo. At one of these early rodeos the arena director rode over to Earl and his older brother, who were standing in front of the chutes, and he said, "You kids had better get back over the fence so you won't get hurt." "But Sir" the boys pleaded, "We've entered the bronc riding." The arena director stared at them with his mouth aghast. "What's the matter, sir? The boys asked don't you leave us?" "I can't make up my mind, he confessed."

Ray Knight used to like to see us ride his big broncs, Earl remembers. "The higher they threw us the wider he grinned." "Ray said, you boys can practice on any Bronc I have." Earl recalled that on one roundup they gather 1,200 horses and bucked them out over the next two weeks.

Saddle Bronc Riding

Ray Knight and a partner, Mr. Ad Day, had formed a rodeo stock contracting company called the Knight and Day Stampedes. Some of his infamous bucking horses weighed over 1,500 pounds and many become world renowned bucking horse. They were seen in big rodeos held at Calgary, Pendleton, New York and Chicago. Horses like Slim Sweden, Easy Money, Box Car, Wild Boy, Jack Dempsey, Horned Toad, Hotshot, Spot-On-The-Belly (later named War Paint) and Reservation (later called No Name). Earl vividly recalled, Wild

Boy, who weighed 1,700 pounds and could split a saddle in two, and Slim Sweden who took the famous bronc rider, Pete Knight, to the pay window at Calgary. Pete Knight was not related Ray Knight. Earl was the first person to ever ride Slim Sweden in a professional rodeo; that was back in 1931; Earl said that he remembered that he bucked off right at the 8 second whistle. He really respected Slim Sweden.

His brother, Mel, later rode him to a championship at Lethbridge, Alberta. Earl rodeoed for 22 years and traveled the rodeo circuit with his three brothers -- Raymond (often call Tom after Tom mix), Mel, and Weldon. Sometimes they traveled with the Lybbert boys and the Lund boys.

In 1931 at the Stirling, Alberta Stampede, Earl entertained the crowd as a Rodeo Clown and he combined that with some of the riding events. As far as history shows, he was the first Canadian rodeo clown ever. He later clowned and fought bulls for the McBride Rodeo Company.

The years 1935, 36, 37, saw Earl and his brother Weldon and some other Canadian cowboys – Mel and Jake Lybbert, Salty Ross and "Suicide" Ted Elder - put on the first rodeos in the state of Mississippi. Earl was the director of these rodeos. It was there in Mississippi that Earl met a young Southern U.S. girl who later became his wife.

During his rodeo years Earl won several all-around championships. Probably his best year was 1933. He competed well in saddle bronc riding, bull riding and bareback. In the steer decorating event he had a real hot streak, later being crowned the reserve Champion at the North American Championship contest at the Calgary Stampede. He broke the world record at the Lethbridge Stampede and set a new arena record at the Raymond Stampede. Earl won money and every rodeo he entered in that event and was awarded third place in the world standings by the Rodeo Association of America.

As a member of the Rodeo Historical Society, Earl Bascom is known in rodeo history as the inventor of two important pieces of rodeo equipment. In 1922, he designed and made rodeo's first hornless bronc saddle, which everyone called the "Mulee." [See page 122] It was first used at the Cardston, Alberta Stampede. In 1924, he designed and made the first one - handed bareback rigging. And that

119

rigging was first used by Earl at the Raymond, Alberta Stampede. Today these two items are standard equipment are used at all professional rodeos throughout United States and Canada.

For his contributions to the sport of rodeo, Earle was awarded honorary membership in the Professional Rodeo Cowboys Association and the Canadian Rodeo Cowboys Association. He was also an early member of the Cowboys Turtle Association, the forerunner organization to the P.R.C.A. as it is known today.

Earl showed an early interest and talent in art, but art training in the one-room, school that consisted of grades 1 through 12; was as rare as his attendance. In 1919, while working for the 5H Ranch, he got into trouble with the Canadian Mounted Police for truancy. Earle hadn't been in school for a couple of years. He felt that going all way through grade three was enough. Besides, he could read all there was to read in the weekly newspaper. That is if he wanted to. Even though Earl thought he was all finished with his schooling, the Mountie (Policeman) marched him back to the schoolhouse.

He felt better about the whole deal when he got a job driving an old stagecoach to and from school. It was used as a school bus by the local school district and his job was to pick up the kids at the various ranches along the way. Earl was 13 years old at the time and was already a well experience teamster. Why? Because Earl's first job as a teamster was in 1916, he drove a four horse team all spring and summer for the Bar N outfit. That job required that he worked all alone, cooking his own meals - he was only nine years old.

All these experiences enter into Earl's artwork. The first time Earl's natural talent with recognized was during a contest at the one-room school. There actually were two contests. The first was a contest to determine the best penmanship. Earl was voted unanimously as the worst in the whole school. Then his teacher brought in a live duck and the contest was to draw the best duck. Earl was voted the best artist. The second time Earl's talent was recognized was when he drew an 'almost – masterpiece' on the papered wall of the family home.

"No picture I ever painted kicked up as much fuss as that one did"; he recalled.

Desiring to be an artist, he filled the empty pages of his school books and other piece of paper with scenes of roundups and cattle

120

drives. Having seen the artwork of C. M. Russell helped inspire Earl to want to be an artist. Charlie Russell actually visited the Kirkcaldy Ranch several times while Earl was worked there. Charlie Russell painted a picture of Ray Knight. But Earl never got to meet Russell personally. This painting of Russell's hung in Ray Knight's front room and showed Ray busting a steer while riding his favorite horse, Bluebird. It was dated 1918. The horse bridle shown in the painting was silver mounted. Ray Knight gave that same bridle to Earl as payment for breaking several horses for him.

About this time, Earl got real fired up about the idea of being an artist and so with a few extra bucks in my pocket for breaking some colts, he sent away for a well advertised correspondence art course from some company in New York. But he soon learned that punching cows from dawn to dark and finding time to do art lessons just didn't mix.

A later event turned his thoughts more seriously towards art. While riding towards town, his horse spooked, then attempted to jump a mud puddle only to slip and flip completely over. Earl said he thought every bone in his body was broken. Luckily he was only bruised and dazed. Earl made his way to the Hicken place to recuperate. Earl began to realize that an accident like that good get very serious. One of the Hicken boys had recently returned from Utah where he was attending the Brigham Young University. He encouraged Earl to pursue some art training at B.Y.U. and develop his talent.

Art is what Earl wanted, and with a successful summer of rodeoing, he had enough money to give it a try. So Earl quit punching cows and traded his rawhide lariat for a chance at a college baccalaureate. College wasn't easy for Earl - he hadn't even graduate from high school. He confesses there he was a 27-year-old freshman and he hadn't been to school in years. He felt like a wild horse in a pen.

It took seven years with a few interruptions and a lot of persistence to finally graduate, for example one year he quit. In 1934 right in the middle of the semester he quit to go to England. He was one of 12 top Canadian cowboys chosen to enter a world championship rodeo in London, England; but he missed the boat. His brother, Weldon, made over there. Also three more rodeos in

Mississippi interrupted his schooling for a while. But he wanted to be an artist, so he never gave up. Eventually he took every art class available at the University. He studied painting, drawing, sculpture and etching while at B.Y.U. His efforts paid off as in his freshman year he won the Studio Guild Award for the best oil painting of the year.

In order to finance his tuition, board and room, and art supplies, he rodeoed at all summer long, between school semesters. All contests he entered were professional -- no amateur rodeos. You had to be good to win and you had to win to keep going. Earl Bascom earned the title, "Rodeos First Collegiate Cowboy" being the first man and perhaps the only man to finance his way through college solely by riding in professional rodeos.

After graduation in 1940, California became the home for Earl and his wife, Nadine, and family. In California Earl got into the construction business, yet they lived on a small cattle ranch. He played the part of an outlaw in the Hollywood movie "Lawless Rider", he was a high school art teacher, and worked with Roy Rogers in TV commercials -- all the time during his artwork.

Rodeo's First Hornless Saddle - 1922

Noted for his accomplishments in the rodeo art fields he is listed in the Who's Who in the American art, Who's Who in the West, and Who's Who in California. Earl Bascom's art is found in many international collections both public and private.

122

Earl's art shows that he was well acquainted with his subject matter. He often said, "It is the life of the cowboy I come to know. I have ridden and broken to ride hundreds of wild horses. I've chased wild horses in the Badlands of Utah, Colorado, Montana and Canada. I have ridden on horse roundups and cattle roundups and branded hundred calves. I've made saddles, stirrups, chaps, spurs, bridles and bits, ropes and hackamores, and patched my own boots." Very few western artists have ever had such a wide variety of cowboy experiences as the cowboy of cowboy artists -- Earl W. Bascom.

Common Western Terms and Words
and What they Mean

Blow-up - 1. Any time a horse begins to violently buck and carry on without prior notice or provocation they are said to "blow-up". Similar terms are to "turn on", "fire", and "come unwound". Now as far as doing so without prior notice seasoned horsemen most of the time read can sense a horse's feelings such that they can be forewarned. Often a good horseman is well enough warned that he can prevent a horse from "blowing up". For example if a cowboy senses that a horse is about to buck he can often avert such action by cueing the horse into a turn. Sometimes just a soft spoken word or two will do. On the other hand however, in a bronc riding event at a rodeo a cowboy wants the bronc to fire, blow-up, come unwound, or come unglued such that should the cowboy make a successful ride he'll score higher.

Bronc - 1. A bronc is simply an untrained horse or a colt. 2. A bronc is a bucking horse that loves to buck and strongly resists training. 3. A bronc usually belongs to a rodeo bucking string of horses. Real western folk do NOT use the term BRONKO or BRONCO.

Brood - 1. A small number of chicks that have been hatched by a Hen and are now following that mother hen. For example: The little Red Hen had a brood of 8 chicks.

Bunch - 1. A number of things grouped or held together. 2. Not a full herd of cattle, horses or sheep rather a smaller group. He found a bunch of cows in a small coulee.

Bull - 1. A mature male animal that has NOT been castrated and is allowed, indeed encouraged, to breed and impregnate cows. In these stories bulls are bovine, not Deer or Elk.

Cattle- 1. Another word for cows. Usually plural – anything from a small bunch to a large herd of cattle.

124

Castrated - 1. A male animal that has had its testicles removed. Castration, castrate; this is the same as neuter or neutered, except neuter refers to male or female. In a strictly female animal it known as spay, they are spayed by removal of the ovaries.

Colt - 1. A colt is a young horse male or female that is still suckling its mother. 2. Colt can also be applied to any young horse up to 1 to 2 years old. 3. A colt is also a term applied to an un-castrated male horse 1 to 3 years old.

Cow - 1. A mature female animal, usually bovine. Cow is also applied to other animals such as elephants and elk and moose.

Draw - 1. The names of bucking horses or bucking bulls are written on small pieces of paper and then put into a hat or bucket and then drawn or pulled out one at a time to determine which rodeo cowboy will ride that particular animal at that rodeo; "Pete Knight drew Slim Sweden in the Saddle Bronc event".

Herd - 1. A group of animals that live or are kept together. 2. A group of animals that have been collected or herded into a group. 3. A gathering of cattle, sheep or horses that have been collected or herded into a group with the intention to herd, chase or move them along as a group from one location to another.

Herded - 1. The act of gathering and keeping cattle, sheep or horses into one group. 2. The process of chasing or herding a group of livestock from one location to another.

Herd Quiter - 1. A horse or cow that suddenly runs away from the herd in an attempt to escape and be by itself.

Herding - 1. See Herd and Herded

Horse - Everyone knows what a horse is right? What about a pickup horse? A pickup horse is a horse ridden by a pickup-man. At the end of an 8 second bronc ride a pickup man reins his pickup horse in along side of the bucking hose so that the bronc rider can get off the bucking horse more safely. Not all horses like getting in that close to a fellow bucking horse. Also a pickup man rides his pickup horse after the ride is over and clears the rodeo arena – that is he chases the bucking horse or bucking bull out of the arena in preparation for the next ride. No pickup men and pickup horses do "NOT" attempt to pickup bull riders from off of bucking bull. This is one reason bull riding is considered more daring. This is where the Rodeo Clowns come in.

Jingle Horse - A jingle horse is a horse used to gather a string of horse or rather the remuda in preparation for the days work. In the early days the remuda was turned loose along with a bell mare. A bell mare (it was usually a mare) is a mare that has a bell strapped to her neck. In the morning when a cowboy or cowboys rode out to gather in the remuda they could hear the bell ringing for miles and thus they knew which direction to ride for the herd. They could hear the jing,le thus they were riding the gathering horse or as it became known the jingle horse. Thus we have the terms jingle pasture or wrangle pasture – these being a set aside pasture for the remuda.

Wrangle horse - the same as a jingle horse.

Packhorses - these are horses usually or strictly used to carry items in a packsaddle.

Draft or work horse - these were large, heavy horses, used for pulling heavy loads such as a load of hay, a horse drawn plow or a rodweeder.

Buggy horse - these were lighter horses used to pull buggies or a winter sleigh.

Us'in horse - Any horse trained enough to be used. Such a term has various conitations.
Note: A Us'in horse to a quite, timid school teacher and rough and tumble cowboy could be two quite different horses.

Hungup - 1. Occasionally a cowboy's boot would not readily slip out of a saddle's stirrup and he would be temporarily hungup in his stirrup and this could cause him to take a bad fall. In some worst cases a cowboy's whole boot (and foot) would slip all the way through the stirrup and sometimes a cowboy would end up being drug or kicked to death. 2. Sometimes it was said hangup.

Remuda - 1. A gathering of horses currently being used to do the day to day work on a ranch. 2. On a large ranch each cowboy will have a remuda, from 2 to 3 head on up to 5 or 6 individual horses. On a large ranch cowboys often ride anywhere from 50 to 100 miles a day and thus do not ride the same horse each day. Once in while they'll ride two horse in the same day. By having a private remuda each horse will get several days rest between long rides. On a large ranch each cowboy would likely ride 15 to 20 different horses though out the year. He'll have a change of remuda for each season, spring, summer, fall and winter. For example a cowboy that rides during the winter while there is lots of snow and snowdrifts to pass through will choose to ride a larger horse.

Rein - 1. Usually plural – that is reins. Reins are used while riding a saddle horse. These are mostly long narrow strips of leather about ½ inch to ¾ in width and 7 to 8 feet long. Sometimes however reins are made of braided cord, webbing or even rope. The reins are connected to the bridle at one end and the other end of the reins are held in the rider's hands, thus giving the rider control over a horse. The reins are used to turn the horse left or right and also bring the horse to a stop. 2. The act of turning a horse left or right or asking the horse to come to a stop. - "He reined his horse to the right and then urged the horse into a lope".

Lines - 1. Mostly plural – that is lines. Lines are used while driving a single horse on a buggy or a team of horses as they pull something. There can be teams of 2, 4 or 6 hoses. Lines are narrow strips of leather about ¾ inch to 1 inch in width and anywhere from 10 to 12 feet long. (Longer for a 4 or 6 horse team) Lines are occasionally made of braided cord or webbing. Lines are connected to the bridle on the single buggy horse or draft horses and the other end of the lines are held by the driver or teamster while sitting on the seat of the wagon. Using the lines the teamster can turn the horses left or right and also bring them to a stop. Lines are like reins on a saddle horse and are used much the same.

Mule   - 1. A Mule is the offspring of a male donkey [Jack] and a female horse. For many years it was believed that a female mule could not get pregnant and have offspring. In now is known that occasionally they can and do get pregnant and have offspring.

Mule Skinner   - 1. A Mule can be ridden like a saddle horse or worked like a workhorse. Mules can be very difficult to handle, especially by inexperienced handlers. Often it was suggested that in order to handle a mule one needed to whip them so severely that the handler caused parts of the mules skin to be removed, thus mule handlers were often deemed to be a muleskinner. Those who were good with livestock soon learned the special methods of handling mules and indeed handled them as easily as horses.

Most Muleskinners handled Mules without any need to whip them or mistreat in any way and yet they were just the same said to be a muleskinner. Some people even used this term for those who drove a team of workhorses.

Snubbing Post - 1. Most early ranches had a corral (often a round corral) mainly used to rope *wild animals and thus near the centre of the corral they would set a large post deep in the ground. Snubbing posts usually stand off the ground 5 to 6 feet. These posts were large in diameter, such as 16 to 20 inches across. After an animal had been roped the roper would take one or two wraps around this snubbing post. These one or two wraps would instantly give the cowboy the advantage. As the wild animal would struggle any time the rope got slack in it the cowboy would take up the slack until eventually the animal would be close enough to pet and train. The snubbing posts also provided some protection for the cowboy should a bull charge him or a bronc attempt to strike at him. Some ranches also used a snubbing pole, some had both.

*The term wild here does not mean wild like a deer, a moose, or a bear but rather an untamed livestock etc.

128

String of Horses - 1. That private remuda or selection of horses a cowboy is currently riding. 2. A string of horses is sometime referred to simply as a string. 3. A ranch will often designate horses as being a string of saddle horses, a string of workhorses, a string of buggy horses and some a string of bucking horses. 4. The word string is used because sometimes when cowboys travelled from one ranch to join cowboys from several other ranches for the fall roundup they took their remuda of horses tied to a long rope. This remuda was said to be lead on a string (long rope) and/or because they travelled in line, one behind the other it was said they were strung out and travelled in or as a string.

Steer Decorating – This was an event that predates Bull Dogging, which in turn predates Steer Wrestling. The Steers used in Steer Decorating were mostly lager than he steers used for Bull Dogging or Steer Wrestling today, also these steers usually had larger and longer horns. Just like the Bull Dogging and Steer Wrestling of today there was a second rider who would ride out the same time as the person who was the contestant, the Decorator, only this second rider rode up on the right side of the steer while the Decorator would ride on the left side of the steer. This second rider's job was to keep the steer running straight down the arena. In as much as the second rider did not make contact with the steer it was said the his job was to haze the steer, hence the second rider became known as the Hazer.

The contestant known as the Decorator would hold an elastic strip, to which a red ribbon was attached. He would hold this strip over the two fingers next to the thumb and also the thumb of his right hand. He would handle the bridle reins with his left hand. Once the Decorator was in what he deemed to be the proper position he was to leave his horse and while hanging on to the steer's left hone; and with his right elbow hugging the steer's neck he would side the elastic strip and red ribbon over the end of the steer's right horn. As soon as he was finished he would throw both hands in the air and the timers would stop their stop watches. If the ribbon feel off the time would not count and the Decorator (contestant) would be disqualified. If the Decorator was to place the ribbon on the horn

129

before both of his feet were on the ground he would also be disqualified and given no time. In the early days of this sport a left handed Decorator could ride up on the steer's right side and the Hazer would ride up on the steer's left side. Not so today in Bull Dogging or Steer Wrestling.